M

D0838987

INSIGHT ⊙ GUIDES

EXPLORE

# SINGAPORE

668

APR 02 2019

# ⊙ Walking Eye App

## YOUR FREE EBOOK AVAILABLE THROUGH THE WALKING EYE APP

Your guide now includes a free eBook to your chosen destination, for the same great price as before. Simply download the Walking Eye App from the App Store or Google Play to access your free eBook.

## HOW THE WALKING EYE APP WORKS

Through the Walking Eye App, you can purchase a range of eBooks and destination content. However, when you buy this book, you can download the corresponding eBook for free. Just see below in the grey panel where to find your free content and then scan the QR code at the bottom of this page.

**Destinations:** Download essential destination content featuring recommended sights and attractions, restaurants, hotels and an A–Z of practical information, all available for purchase.

**Ships:** Interested in ship reviews? Find independent reviews of river and ocean ships in this section, all available for purchase.

**eBooks:** You can download your free accompanying digital version of this guide here. You will also find a whole range of other eBooks, all available for purchase.

**Free access to travel-related blog articles** about different destinations, updated on a daily basis.

## HOW THE EBOOKS WORK

The eBooks are provided in EPUB file format. Please note that you will need an eBook reader installed on your device to open the file. Many devices come with this as standard, but you may still need to install one manually from Google Play.

The eBook content is identical to the content in the printed guide.

## HOW TO DOWNLOAD THE WALKING EYE APP

1. Download the Walking Eye App from the App Store or Google Play.
2. Open the app and select the scanning function from the main menu.
3. Scan the QR code on this page – you will then be asked a security question to verify ownership of the book.
4. Once this has been verified, you will see your eBook in the purchased ebook section, where you will be able to download it.

Other destination apps and eBooks are available for purchase separately or are free with the purchase of the Insight Guide book.

915,957
Insight
2019

# CONTENTS

## ARCHITECTURE

Don't miss grand colonial-era buildings in the Civic District (route 1), skyscrapers designed by superstar architects in Marina Bay (route 3), or flamboyant Peranakan terrace houses in Emerald Hill (route 7).

# RECOMMENDED ROUTES FOR...

## THE ARTS

Take in a music or theatre performance at The Esplanade – Theatres on the Bay (route 3), spot public sculptures in the CBD (route 5), and sample Southeast Asian art in the Singapore Art Museum (route 2).

## FOODIES

Food-lovers won't be disappointed with the Singapore-style seafood in the East Coast (route 15) and the hawker offerings at Maxwell Food Centre and Chinatown Food Street (route 6).

## LOCAL CULTURE

Explore the city's eclectic cultures in its ethnic neighbourhoods (routes 6 and 9). For a glimpse into the Straits Chinese way of life, wander around Katong (route 15) or visit the Peranakan Museum (route 2).

## NIGHTLIFE

Flashy clubs at Clarke Quay (route 4) and Marina Bay Sands (route 3) are great for all-night partying. Sentosa (route 11) has laid-back beach bars and jazz fans should head to Bali Lane at Kampong Glam (route 9).

## PARKS AND GARDENS

Opt for a leisurely walk in Gardens by the Bay (route 3), or wander in the landscaped Botanic Gardens before checking out the wonders of the National Orchid Garden (route 8).

## SHOPAHOLICS

Mall-hop on Orchard Road (route 7), browse idiosyncratic shops in Kampong Glam (route 9), comb Chinatown (route 6) and Little India (route 10) for cultural finds, and splurge at VivoCity (route 14).

## WILDLIFE

The city's excellent zoos and safaris boast naturalistic habitats with a focus on conservation. You should absolutely set aside a day for Singapore Zoo, River Safari and Night Safari (route 18).

# INTRODUCTION

An introduction to Singapore's geography, customs and culture, plus illuminating background information on cuisine, history and what to do when you're there.

*Chinatown's night market from above*

# EXPLORE SINGAPORE

*The small city–island state of Singapore has achieved much and has even grander ambitions, but its most distinct joys are to be found in its warm, eclectic people, ethnic neighbourhoods, and the pleasure afforded by its food culture, shopping and nightlife.*

For some, Singapore is merely a welcome stopover, with its top-rated airport making it the perfect gateway to Southeast Asia. For others, this tiny island, with its legendary cleanliness, widespread use of English and celebrated sights, shops, eateries and colourful ethnic neighbourhoods, is an appealing destination in its own right. Indeed, Singapore is an ideal introduction, in fact, to all of Asia in one fell swoop.

## DEVELOPMENT

In 1819, Englishman Thomas Stamford Raffles from the British East India Company recognised the potential of this tiny island. At the time, it was shrouded in jungle and swamp, occupied only by Orang Laut (Sea People), a few Malay families and some Chinese traders. Raffles ordered the land to be cleared, oversaw an ambitious construction campaign and brought labourers and merchants from China, India and all over Southeast Asia to set up a trading post. His free-trade policies soon created a thriving port town of around 10,000 residents.

In short, Raffles can confidently be described as the founding father of modern-day Singapore: both his energy and foresight are embedded in the cultural DNA of this city-state.

### Modern-day Singapore

Singapore owes much of its success to the visionary leadership of visionary Lee Kuan Yew (1923–2015), the country's first prime minister (from 1958 to 1990). Under the direction of Yew and his successors, Goh Chok Tong and Lee Hsien Loong, Singapore has continued to flourish as one of Southeast Asia's brightest stars. The government's paternal approach has defused racial and labour disputes, whereas its public housing schemes have provided most citizens with their own homes. In turn, savvy economic policies have attracted foreign trade and investment.

Invasive socialengineering policies – from banning smoking in public places, the outlawing of the sale of chewing gum, the monitoring of flushing in public toilets to the imposition of punitive taxes on car ownership – may have drawn sneers from

*The Raffles statue*                                    *At a Grand Prix concert*

**Having a Singapore Sling at the Raffles.** This famous cocktail packs a delightful fruity punch. After a hot day in the sun, sip the iconic, chilled concoction at Raffles Hotel's Long Bar, where the drink was created in 1910. See page 37.

**Discovering Peranakan culture.** Learn more about the Peranakan or Straits Chinese culture at the Peranakan Museum, where lavish artefacts and exhibits are presented. Experience more of this unique culture over at East Coast Road, a veritable living museum dotted with Peranakan restaurants and cultural galleries. Don't forget to try some colourful, steamed Nonya cakes. See page 40.

**Strolling around Gardens by the Bay.** The sprawling gardens are home to two massive conservatories filled with lush greenery as well as a dozen Super Trees. The Singapore Garden Festival held here showcases creations by international acclaimed garden and floral designers. Look out for other creative, seasonal floral exhibits such as Tulipmania. See page 47.

**Cruising down the river in a bumboat.** Hop on a bumboat which takes you down the Singapore River. Enjoy views of gleaming skyscrapers juxtaposed with colonial-era buildings, restored conservation warehouses, historical bridges, and riverside sculptures. See page 48.

**Exploring ethnic neighbourhoods.** The eclectic ethnic districts of Chinatown, Kampong Glam and Little India are microcosms of multicultural Singapore. Put on your walking shoes and soak up their colourful atmospheres on foot. Sample some authentic local cuisines in between your trails. See pages 70 and 74.

**Tucking into chilli crab.** In the food haven of Singapore, one would be hard pressed to name its national dish, but the spicy-sweet chili crab is one of the strongest contenders. Among the best places to savour this dish are the restaurants at the East Coast Centre. See page 119.

**Prowling with nocturnal animals.** A diverse range of animals roams freely in the subtly lit and naturalistic enclosures of the Night Safari. This is a rare chance to catch creatures that are active only at night. But before it turns dark, visit River Safari, where two of China's giant pandas have made their home. See page 99.

**Soaking in the views at the Sands SkyPark.** Head up to the highest level at Marina Bay Sands to take snapshots of the city. There is an observation deck, landscaped gardens and a one-of-a-kind infinity pool with amazing views of the skyline. See page 47.

**Christmas at Orchard Road.** Between November and December, this whole stretch is illuminated with sparkling lights and Christmas decorations. Splurge, window shop or simply experience the festive atmosphere at this mile-long shopping belt. See page 60.

*Shoppers at Bugis Junction*

the Western media, but Singapore is undeniably the cleanest and most orderly of all Asian cities. What some Westerners perceive as draconian laws and the authoritarian curtailing of personal freedoms, are regarded by many pragmatic Singaporeans as merely a common-sense approach to running a country.

## ORIENTATION

On a map of any scale, Singapore is just a dot at the southern tip of peninsular Malaysia. Singapore consists of the main island, which is 699 sq km (270 sq miles) in area, and 63 other smaller islands. Most of the main island is less than 15m (50ft) above sea level, whereas the highest point is Bukit Timah Hill, at 163.63m (537ft).

---

### Public housing

In land-scarce Singapore, providing housing for the masses means building skywards. More than 80 percent of Singaporeans own and live in high-rise flats built by the Housing and Development Board. In many other parts of the world, public housing is associated with poverty and social unrest, but not in Singapore. Its public housing programme is in fact one of its finest achievements, with other fast-growing countries seeking to emulate its success.

---

Downtown Singapore remains largely arranged according to the original town plan that Raffles envisioned in 1819. The colonial hub of the city, today's Civic District, is still the heart of the administration, just as it was in Raffles' time. The clamour of Chinatown and the hum of business in the Central Business District around Raffles Place have not diminished. The Muslim area of Kampong Glam and the predominantly Hindu Little India retain their ethnic feel. Chic Orchard Road, a plantation area in colonial times, has been transformed into one of Asia's premier shopping districts.

### Conservation

When Singapore achieved independence in 1965, the economy was in shambolic state. Like many other developing nations, it prioritised urban renewal and economic progress over the protection of historic neighbourhoods and colonial architectural gems, many of which were simply razed. As a result, by the 1970s Singapore had achieved prosperity, but was criticised for its lack of character and culture.

In the 1980s the authorities began to restore buildings in four conservation areas: Boat Quay, Little India, Kampong Glam and Chinatown/Tanjong Pagar. Since then, more temples, buildings, shophouses and warehouses have been spared the wrecking ball. The gentrification, apart from

*Playing draughts in Chinatown*

giving the city added charm, has also helped Singaporeans develop a sense of their own history.

### Garden city

Singapore packs in quite a bit despite its minuscule size. Once you have covered the city centre, venture out to the suburbs, where the housing heartlands are interspersed with quirky theme attractions as well as forest reserves and other pockets of greenery.

The city's vast green zones surprise many first-time visitors, at least those expecting to find a sterile and air-conditioned metropolis of glass and steel. There is a legion of green belts, such as parks nestled between skyscrapers, offering respite in the concrete jungle. Four gazetted nature reserves – Central Catchment, Bukit Timah, Sungei Buloh and Labrador – together comprise over 3,340 hectares (8,250 acres) of untouched greenery, which is by no means slim pickings for this land-scarce city.

### Getting around

Street signs are clear and the city is relatively easy to navigate. The various districts can be easily explored by bus, Mass Rapid Transit (MRT) trains or on foot, although the weather can get hot, humid and possibly uncomfortable for some. Taxis are comfortable, inexpensive and especially good for journeys to destinations in the suburbs.

## MELTING POT

Singapore is home to about 5.8 million people, comprising 76.2 percent Chinese, 13.3 percent Malays, 7.2 percent Indians, with the small remaining figure made up of Eurasians, Arabs, Jews and other minority groups.

The lingua franca is English, but on the streets you will see Chinese, Malay, Indian, Eurasian and Caucasian faces. Singapore has been a migrant society since day one, and continues to receive new immigrants from all over the world. Mosques, churches, and Hindu and Chinese temples often stand side by side, and cuisines borrow ideas and ingredients from one another. Indeed, fusion is very much the order of the day.

Four official languages are used in multicultural Singapore: English, Mandarin, Malay and Tamil, with English the official language of administration. On the streets, you will hear different languages and dialects being spoken, including Singlish, a patois that combines English, Malay and Chinese dialects, which most Singaporeans closely identify with.

### Preoccupations

The country tends to be overly competitive, thanks to a *kiasu* (meaning 'afraid to lose' in the Chinese Hokkien dialect) attitude. Singapore is always in a big hurry to chase grand

*East coast café life*

dreams and strive for success, and has already made itself the world's busiest port and the second largest oil refiner, as well as home to what is often voted the globe's best airline and airport. The ambition to be No. 1 in everything it does is perhaps driven by a sense of insecurity and the need to get the attention of and connect to the world beyond its limited shores, though the positive result of this is that the city has become a well-oiled, efficient machine.

Keeping up with the Joneses is also a major preoccupation of Singaporeans. At housewarming parties queries about the cost of the house and renovation are earnestly entertained. A compliment on a nice watch or a piece of jewellery will almost always be followed by a question on its price and provenance. If you are asked questions on money, don't be fazed; no rudeness or intrusiveness is intended.

### Pastimes

When removed from their workaday world and indulging in their favourite pastimes, Singaporeans do inlet up and have fun. Without a doubt, the best-loved activity is eating. The island's cultural diversity has given it a mind-boggling array of food options; as a result, this city never stops eating, even into the wee hours of the morning. Shopping ranks only a close second as Singaporeans' favourite diversion. Many indefatigable locals have been known to trawl Orchard Road on the weekends, mall by mall.

## A CHANGING CITY

Singaporeans joke that if they leave the country for more than three months, they will not be able to recognise many places on their return, so relentless is the pace of the city's transformation. Indeed, today the city is undergoing a flourishing of epic proportions. A new financial district and a revitalised waterfront has given it an extra boost and tourist arrivals have been increasing, especially thanks to the opening of two casino resorts – known as Integrated Resorts – and a Universal Studios theme park. There were concerns that the casinos in these resorts would encourage gambling, so Lee Hsien Loong suggested that safeguards should be put in place. As a result, Singaporeans and permanent residents pay an entrance fee of S$100 per visit or S$2,000 annually.

The city, once derided as boring, is also learning to take itself less seriously. Its nightlife scene pulses with cool bars and clubs, both imported and home-grown; you'll also find a heavenly range of cuisines here. And if the vibrant arts calendar is anything to go by, its appetite for high culture is definitely growing. Singapore is having fun, and everywhere you go there is a plethora of things to do and see.

*In the heart of Chinatown*

## TOP TIPS FOR VISITING SINGAPORE

**Child's play.** The Jacob Ballas Children's Garden (Tue–Sun 8am–7pm; free), in the Botanic Garden's Bukit Timah Core, is a playground and nature park for kids. Adults can enter only if accompanied by a child below 13 years old or by a guide. At the zoo's Rainforest Kidzworld (daily 9am–5.30pm), children can hop on animal rides, run loose at a water playground and watch animal shows.

**Festive seasons.** October or November is one of the best times to visit Little India, as the whole place is dressed and lit for the Festival of Lights celebrations. In September and October every year, Chinatown and the Chinese Garden at Jurong are ablaze with pretty lanterns for the annual Mid-Autumn Festival celebrations.

**Park Hopper.** If you plan to visit the Singapore Zoo, River Safari, Night Safari and Jurong Bird Park, buy multi-park tickets such as the 4-in-1 Park Hopper ticket to get a lower combined price. The ticket is valid for one month from the date of purchase. You may visit each park on a different day. For Park Hopper options with Jurong Bird Park, Singapore Zoo or Night Safari, the ticket prices include tram rides.

**Sentosa entrance fees.** If you take the Sentosa Express to the island, the entrance fee is included in the fare of S\$4. You can also enter the island via Sentosa Express using the ez-link card. If you walk via the Boardwalk, the entrance fee is S\$1. Those who take a taxi will be charged either S\$2, \$3, \$5 or \$6 per taxi depending on the time and day. Most of the individual attractions have separate admission fees, which can add up if you are bringing your family, so take advantage of 'package' tickets with entrance to multiple attractions at discounts. Call 1800-736 8672 or visit www.sentosa.com.sg for more information.

**Pricey booze.** Expect to pay S\$10 or more for a pint of beer and S\$12–14 for house pours. Premium beers cost about S\$15–20 a pop, and a bottle of bubbly around S\$100. All bills are tagged with a 10 percent service charge and 7 percent tax. Take advantage of happy hour discounts or one-for-one deals, usually from 5–9pm.

**Southern Islands overnight.** Those who want to experience an overnight stay on St John's Island can book the Holiday Bungalow, which comes with a kitchen and houses 10 persons; or the Holiday Camp, which can accommodate up to 60 persons. Bookings and immediate payment must be made personally at the Sentosa Express station at VivoCity (tel: 1800-736 8672; daily 9am–8pm). For overnight camping (bring your own equipment) on Sisters' Islands and Pulau Hantu, you must obtain prior approval from Sentosa (email: administrator@sentosa.com.sg). There are no food and drink vendors on the islands, except Kusu during the pilgrimage season. It might be a good idea to pack a picnic when visiting these islands.

*A food festival feast*

# FOOD AND DRINK

*Singapore's cultural diversity has resulted in a vibrant food scene and a veritable explosion of flavours. With a mind-boggling array of options that cater to tastes and budgets, you will never go hungry on this island.*

Eating is a great passion in Singapore and life revolves around food. Singaporeans talk about food all the time and debate on where to get the freshest crabs, the spiciest chilli sauce or the best chicken rice – for hours on end and preferably over a meal. At the many food courts and hawker centres peppered all over the island, you can sample different cuisines in a single venue freshly cooked by an array of vendors.

Every imaginable cuisine is represented on this island, from refined Japanese and piquant Korean to robust Thai and exotic Middle Eastern. There are also excellent fine-dining restaurants, including Modern European, and traditional French and Italian, all with impressive wine lists to match.

## CHINESE CUISINE

For just Chinese cuisine alone, a wide range of authentic restaurants can be found in Singapore – including those that serve the regional cuisines of China and specialties of different ethnic groups.

Delicate dim sum, double-boiled soups and roasted meats are prepared in the Cantonese kitchen, while hearty meat dishes are rustled up by Hokkien cooks. Refined Teochew dishes usually comprise light, wholesome flavours such as steamed seafood, comforting rice porridge and clear soups. The Hakkas are famous for their *yong tau fu* or bean curd stuffed with fish paste, and home-spun dishes flavoured with potent home-made rice wine.

The tongue-numbing Sichuan and robust Hunan food, both known for their liberal use of hot chilli peppers, as well as strongly flavoured Shanghainese and fine Beijing dishes are some of the many regional cuisines one can savour here.

## INDIAN CUISINE

The Indian kitchen is largely divided into South and North Indian. South Indian meals mainly consist of fiery curries, aromatic *biryani* rice cooked with meat or seafood, as well as vegetarian *thosai* (rice pancakes) served with lentils. Several Indian restaurants in Singapore are well known for serving spicy southern fare on banana leaves.

North Indian cuisine is famous for its flavoursome tandoor grills, mild and rich

*Chicken satay is a favourite*

*Laksa, a typical local dish*

curries, as well as fluffy *naan* breads. Meanwhile, the Keralan table, although not as well known, features a host of lip-smacking seafood dishes.

Indian chefs often use a blend of spices such as cardamom, cloves, cumin and coriander to enliven their dishes. Yoghurt is sometimes added to North Indian curries to temper the spices, whereas coconut milk is used to mellow the intensely hot South Indian ones.

A hybrid Indian-Muslim food is usually found in hawker stalls around the island. Some familiar specialities are *roti prata* (a flaky griddle-fried bread eaten with curry), as well as *murtabak* (like *roti prata*, but stuffed with shredded chicken or mutton, sliced onions and egg).

## MALAY CUISINE

Singaporean Malays are descendants of settlers from the Malayan Peninsula or Indonesia's Java and Sumatra islands. Mention Malay cuisine and one usually thinks of *nasi padang* (rice and assorted meat and vegetable side dishes) and spicy curries. These dishes usually include an assortment of spices and herbs such as ginger, turmeric, galangal, lemongrass, curry leaves, chillies and the ubiquitous *belacan* (a pungent shrimp paste). These dishes are often balanced with coconut milk, which takes the edge off the heat.

*Nasi padang* originates from Padang in West Sumatra. The many *nasi padang* eateries dotted around the island usu-

ally offer a wide variety of spicy meat and vegetable dishes served with white or turmeric-flavoured rice. At hawker centres, visit Malay stalls for the perennial favourite, satay. Aromatic bamboo skewers of marinated beef, mutton or chicken are grilled over hot charcoal and served with sliced onion, cucumber, rice cakes and a piquant spicy and sweet peanut sauce.

## PERANAKAN CUISINE

A unique cuisine that deserves special mention is Peranakan, or Nyonya, cooking. Peranakans are descendants of early immigrants from China who settled in 19th-century Penang, Melaka and Singapore and married local Malay women. Per-

## Cookery classes

There are two established cookery schools in Singapore that really stand out from the crowd. At-Sunrice GlobalChef Academy (28 Tai Seng Street, Lift Lobby 2, Level 5; www.at-sunrice.com) offers demonstrations, tasting classes and hands-on cooking classes in Asian cuisine. Palate Sensations (Chromos #01-03, 10 Biopolis Road (opposite Buona Vista MRT and MOE Building); www.palatesensations.com) is an open concept studio offering a range of hands-on cooking classes. Asian, Italian, Chinese and French cuisines are taught by the resident executive chef and other guest chefs.

*Tempting crispy prawns*

anakan cuisine originates from the fusion of Malay and Chinese culinary styles.

To impart a distinctive flavour and aroma to their rich curries and stews, chefs add the essential *rempah* mixture – fragrant herbs and spices such as lemongrass, chillies, shallots, candlenuts, *belacan* (shrimp paste) and turmeric ground by hand in a pestle and mortar. Tamarind paste, coconut milk and *taucheo* (fermented beans) are also used to liven up the robust concoctions. Dishes often require long hours of slow cooking and complicated preparations; flavours are complex and can range from fiery to delicate.

Desserts – in the form of little cakes called *nyonya kueh* – are colourful, sweet and sticky: perfumed with coconut cream and pandan leaves, and sweetened with dark and syrupy palm sugar.

Although best eaten in a Peranakan home, this cooking can be enjoyed in a handful of restaurants in Singapore. Look out for dishes such as *ayam buah keluak*, which combines chicken with earthy Indonesian black nuts to produce a rich, thick gravy as well as beef *rendang*, a spicy, dry beef stew that is often simmered for hours until fork tender.

## SINGAPORE'S SIGNATURE DISHES

Over the years, several unique delicacies have evolved to tantalise the local taste buds. These dishes are particularly close to the hearts of Singaporeans.

### Hainanese chicken rice

This iconic dish was first introduced by Hainanese immigrants from China. Succulent and juicy chicken meat poached in stock is served with fragrant rice that has been steamed with ginger, garlic and chicken stock. The chicken and rice are then served with delicious dips – vinegary chilli sauce, ginger paste and sweet black soy sauce.

### Fish-head curry

This speciality is unique to the Indian community. Massive fish heads are stewed in a gravy alongside eggplant, tomatoes and okra. The meat is succulent and the gravy, spicy and intense. Aficionados say the cheeks, lips and eyes are the best parts of the fish head.

### Chilli crab

Singaporeans will tell you that this dish is best made with giant Sri Lankan crabs. The thick, tangy and spicy gravy is mopped up with fried or steamed *mantou* (Chinese buns).

### Laksa

Thick rice noodles bathed in a rich and spicy coconut gravy jazzed up with herbs, and crowned with sliced fish cake, tofu, cockles, prawns and beansprouts.

## BREAKFAST

A typical Singaporean breakfast usually means heading to a coffee shop for a dose of freshly grilled *kaya* toast

*Lau Pa Sat Festival Market*

– bread spread with butter and a sweet coconut jam made from sugar, eggs and coconut cream, and flavoured with pandan leaves. To complement the stacks of crispy *kaya* toast, one can also order soft-boiled eggs drizzled with soy sauce and a cup of thick black coffee.

## DRINKS AND DESSERTS

An iconic drink is *teh tarik* or 'pulled tea'. Tea sweetened with condensed milk is poured from cup to pitcher and back again to ensure that the concoction is well mixed and frothy. A variation is the soothing *teh halia* or ginger tea, a staple at Indian drink vendors. In hawker centres and at food courts, try freshly squeezed fruit juice, cold soya bean milk or sugar cane juice served with a wedge of lemon.

Delicious food needs something worthy to wash it down with, and the locally brewed Tiger and Anchor beers are excellent choices. Don't leave without tasting a Singapore Sling – a zesty blend of gin, cherry brandy, Cointreau, pineapple juice and fresh lime.

To end your meal, try *cendol* or ice *kacang* – shaved iced desserts with red beans and jelly, topped with syrup and coconut milk or evaporated milk.

## HAWKER CENTRES

Hawker centres are scattered all over the island. Always a hive of activity, the scores of Malay, Chinese and Indian stalls offer a wide variety of traditional fare at low prices that will not break the bank. Some of the most popular hawker centres are Lau Pa Sat Festival Market, Maxwell Road Food Centre and Newton Food Centre. From dawn until dusk, row upon row of stalls bustle with hawkers dishing out their specialities. Regulars often throng these places in search of their favourite stalls. Every evening, Boon Tat Street beside the Lau Pa Sat Festival Market becomes a pedestrian-only street and is transformed into an atmospheric haunt for satay lovers. Hawkers grill skewered meat over burning charcoal and serve them with rice cakes and a tangy peanut sauce dip.

The local hawker centres are always packed during lunch and dinner, so head there earlier if you don't have the patience or time to wait for a table. However, communal sharing of tables is common during busy hours – simply smile and ask the person at the table if you can share it. If you are with a group at a hawker centre, have one person sit at a table to reserve the seats. The others, having noted the table number, should order their food and tell the hawkers where they are seated.

## Food and drink prices

Price guide for a meal for one (excluding drinks and taxes):
$$$$ = over S$60
$$$ = S$40–60
$$ = S$20–40
$ = below S$20

*Luxury boutiques at ION Orchard*

# SHOPPING

*Singapore's shopping scene is red-hot. New malls sprout at breakneck speed while older ones receive makeovers. The choice ranges from Orchard Road's shiny, glitzy shopping centres to charming shophouses in the ethnic enclaves.*

Shops in Singapore are generally open daily from 10–11am to about 9pm, so you can literally shop till you drop. Some shopping centres on Orchard Road open until late on Friday and Saturday nights. Although there are no distinct sales periods that follow the seasons, stores generally mark down their prices periodically. The best time to shop is from late May to early July during the annual Great Singapore Sale. You'll also find great bargains post-Christmas and in and around the Chinese New Year.

Note that there is a 7 percent Goods and Services Tax (GST) on most purchases in Singapore, for which tourists can claim a refund for purchases above S$100 at the airport before departure.

## SHOPPING DISTRICTS

### Orchard Road
Orchard Road is to Singapore what Fifth Avenue is to New York. Even people who have never been to Singapore have heard of Orchard Road, such is its claim to shopping fame. The area is a shopaholic's dream – one dazzling mall after another filled with swanky department stores and any number of retail outlets and designer boutiques. There are malls dedicated to young children (Forum The Shopping Mall), adolescents (Far East Plaza), antique and carpet fiends (Tanglin Shopping Centre) and the moneyed (Hilton Gallery, ION Orchard, Ngee Ann City and The Paragon), along with the usual shopping centres selling all manner of goods.

### Marina Bay
The mega-sized Suntec City Mall has countless shops selling clothes, shoes, bags, electronic equipment, books and sports apparel. Adjoining it is a subterranean shopping mall called CityLink Mall, which conveniently connects to the City Hall MRT station, Marina Square and the Esplanade Mall, part of the Esplanade – Theatres on the Bay.

The Shoppes at Marina Bay Sands boasts over 800,000 square feet of retail and restaurant space. You can indulge in a unique luxury shopping experience here; brands include Hermès, Chanel, Prada and Gucci.

### Civic District
Above the City Hall MRT station is Raffles City, a six-storey mall with a wide

*Souvenir shopping in Chinatown*

array of retail outlets. Just opposite on North Bridge Road is Raffles Hotel Shopping Arcade, with a clutch of designer boutiques.

### Kampong Glam

Arab Street is where to go for fabrics and handwoven baskets. The shops here are piled high with leather bags, baskets and rattan goods, purses and shoes. Haji Lane, lined with vintage boutiques and local designers' shops, is one of Singapore's hippest shopping streets.

### Little India

Serangoon Road and the neighbouring side streets are a treasure trove of spices, jewellery, Indian silk and more from the subcontinent. Mustafa Centre at Syed Alwi Road is a large 24-hour shopping mall crammed with low-priced electronic goods and other bargains. Little India Arcade comprises colourful restored shophouses packed with interesting paraphernalia.

### Chinatown

For all things Chinese, visit the tiny shops along Pagoda Street and Temple Street, and the stalls at the Chinatown Night Market. Nearby Yue Hwa Emporium sells exquisite Chinese silk and handicrafts like teapots and fans.

## WHAT TO BUY

When it comes to purchasing photographic equipment, prices are fairly attractive; but it's best to get an international guarantee. If you want to take a risk on imported goods intended only for the local market, you can save on the price. However, the law comes down hard on bootleg software and frequent raids are carried out at shopping malls specialising in computers – so buy the genuine article and ask for a guarantee.

Watches are sold tax-free, and the choice is endless. Gold jewellery is also a good buy. Traditional designs crafted in 22K yellow gold are available at jewellers on Serangoon Road and in Chinatown, while more contemporary pieces in 18K white or yellow gold, set with precious or semi-precious stones, are sold at local chains like Goldheart and Lee Hwa in the shopping centres. International jewellers like Tiffany and Cartier also have boutiques in Singapore. More unique are orchid blooms – sold under the Risis brand – plated with 22K gold to preserve their beauty and crafted into jewellery.

Home-grown fashion designer Ashley Isham has his own plush store at Mandarin Gallery and Fullerton Square. Other local names of note are projectshopbloodbros, M)Phosis and Bodynits.

The range of antiques and handicrafts from Bangkok, Borneo and beyond is vast. There are baskets from the Philippines, Buddha images from Myanmar, Indian brassware, Chinese ceramics and more. Remember to always ask for a certificate of authenticity.

*Live music at Blu Jaz Cafe*

# ENTERTAINMENT

*Once described as bland and banal, the island's nightlife scene has gone up a few hip notches in recent years. Whether you want to catch a live show, have a no-holds-barred night of bar-crawling, or go clubbing, the choices are plentiful.*

Party-goers in Singapore are a capricious lot, reflected in the overwhelming variety and venues that open (and close) at a furious rate, though established hotspots continue to pack in the crowds, year after year.

## WHERE TO GO

Nightspots are scattered all over the island, but there are a few key areas where you can spend an entire night hopping from one venue to another:

**Singapore River**: The nightlife hubs along the river are a quick taxi ride from one another. The bars and pubs set in conservation shophouses on Boat Quay are popular with tourists and executives from nearby Raffles Place. Upriver from Boat Quay, Clarke Quay sizzles with party-goers in the flashy bars and clubs set in restored 19th-century warehouses.

**Orchard Road**: The main shopping strip of Orchard Road is home to classy hotel lounges and bars with live performances. At its southern end is Emerald Hill, which has charming pubs patronised by expats and creative types.

**Chinatown**: A few streets in Chinatown area buzz with hip independent bars. These include Keong Saik Road, Jiak Chuan Road, and the ever popular Club Street and Ann Siang Hill.

**Sentosa and surroundings**: The beachside bars dotted on the island resort of Sentosa, such as Tanjong Beach Club, are fantastic places for knocking back cocktails. Opposite Sentosa and adjacent to VivoCity shopping mall is St James Power Station, a massive entertainment complex housed in a former coal-fired power station.

**Further afield**: A number of relaxing drinking holes are also worth exploring in more secluded enclaves. One prime example is Dempsey Hill, located near Singapore Botanic Gardens, where you will find some stylish al fresco bars and restaurants housed in former British army barracks and set amid lush greenery.

## HOTEL BARS

If you don't fancy a noisy street of bars and clubs, hotel bars are good alternatives. Swissôtel the Stamford has the

*Singapore is home to some excellent clubs*

vertigo-inducing New Asia Bar on its 71st floor, while Raffles Hotel's Long Bar is the progenitor of the gin-based Singapore Sling. Another good option is the smart Post Bar at the Fullerton Hotel; its menu includes a dizzying array of martinis. The Grand Hyatt's plush Martini Bar is also a top draw for its range of alcoholic concoctions.

## CLUBS

Attica/Attica Too, at Clarke Quay, are home-grown favourites where DJs spin everything from hip-hop to electronic beats. Long-standing club Zouk, a popular clubbing hotspot since 1991, has recently relocated to The Cannery nearby. Most dance clubs have strict dress codes: no slippers, shorts or singlets, and certainly no drugs.

### Gay venues
The pink crowd gather in Tanjong Pagar, where there is a clutch of gay clubs and bars. Popular choices include dance clubs Taboo, and laid-back bars like Tantric and OUT Bar Singapore.

## LIVE ENTERTAINMENT

For such a tiny city, Singapore has a fantastic range of live entertainment.

### Rock and pop music
The best places to listen to Singapore musicians and bands are The Pump Room at Clarke Quay, Timbre @ The Substation and Wala Wala Café Bar in Holland Village. They perform pop and rock covers as well as original works.

### Jazz
For an evening of jazz, head to Boat Quay's Harry's Bar or Arab Street's Blujaz Café. These have line-ups of local bands as well as international jazz acts.

### Classical music
The Singapore Symphony Orchestra performs mainly mainstream classics at their weekly concerts at the Esplanade Concert Hall. Look out, too, for performances at the refurbished Victoria Theatre & Concert Hall.

### Theatre and dance
Singapore's lively English-language theatre scene features a mix of Broadway favourites and musicals, as well as the local productions of original works and international collaborations. Companies include Wild Rice (whose productions have travelled to Wellington, Moscow and Hong Kong), TheatreWorks, The Necessary Stage and Singapore Repertory Theatre.

The dance scene is headlined by the Singapore Dance Theatre, whose repertoire ranges from the classics to contemporary ballet set to pop music. Another company worth checking out is Arts Fission, whose edgy productions draw inspiration from Asian heritage.

*The Chingay parade marks the end of Chinese New Year festivities*

# FESTIVALS AND EVENTS

*Multicultural Singapore is a constant hive of activity, celebrating one festival after another. Almost every month of the year, Singapore's streets, temples and ethnic enclaves come alive with an assortment of religious and cultural celebrations.*

## JANUARY TO MARCH

**Chinese New Year:** The most widely celebrated festival among the Chinese, it falls on the first day of the lunar calendar, usually between mid-January and mid-February. The 15-day festival, beginning with a two-day holiday, is commemorated by feasting and the giving of hong bao, red packets of 'lucky money'. Catch the festive spirit in Chinatown.

**Thaipusam:** This Hindu festival is observed between January and February. Devotees honour Lord Muruga by performing feats of mind over body. The festival begins at dawn at the Srinivasa Perumal Temple in Serangoon Road. Here, devotees who have entered a trance have their bodies pierced with metal hooks or spikes attached to a *kavadi*, a cage-like steel contraption which is carried on their shoulders. The procession makes its way to the Sri Thandayuthapani Temple at Tank Road.

## APRIL TO JUNE

**Vesak Day:** Usually celebrated in May, this is the most important event in the Buddhist calendar, for it honours the birth, death and enlightenment of Buddha. Temple celebrations begin at dawn with a candlelight procession. As part of the celebrations, caged birds are released and free meals are distributed to the poor.

**Dragon Boat Festival:** The festival honours a Chinese patriot, Qu Yuan, who drowned himself in 278 BC as a protest against the corruption of the imperial court. Small packages of rice were thrown into the water to distract fishes from his body, and villagers decorated their boats with dragon heads and tails with the same purpose in mind. Today, several varieties of these rice dumplings are sold at Chinese restaurants and top hotels.

## JULY TO SEPTEMBER

**Singapore Food Festival:** This month-long food fiesta in July holds various food-tasting events and unique dining experiences.

**National Day:** The National Day Parade on 9 August, features pomp and pageantry to celebrate the city-state's independence, and culmi-

*Deepavali Singapore*                    *Singapore National Day flypast*

nates in a stunning fireworks display. Held at the Padang traditionally, National Day is also celebrated at various venues all over Singapore.

**Singapore Night Festival:** For two weekends in August, the art and heritage district of Bras Basah comes alive at night with stunning outdoor illuminations, as well as music, dance, art and aerial performances.

**Singapore International Festival of Arts:** This annual six-week event in August and September showcases a bonanza of Asian and Western performing arts from dance and theatre to music. Past performances have included the Washington Ballet and the London Philharmonic Orchestra.

**Formula 1 Singapore Grand Prix:** This night race held at the Marina Bay area over a weekend in mid-September draws in crowds from all over the world. Besides the world's only night race, there are also plenty of entertainment and concerts held during the Grand Prix season.

## OCTOBER TO DECEMBER

**Mid-Autumn Festival:** This traditional harvest festival takes place on the 15th day of the eighth lunar month, usually in October. Mooncakes – pastries filled with lotus paste or red bean paste – are presented as edible gifts. Don't miss the impressive display of colourful lanterns in Chinatown. There are also street parades.

**Theemithi Festival:** At Sri Mariamman Temple on South Bridge Road, male devotees sprint barefoot across glowing coals in honour of Draupathi, a legendary heroine deified by South Indian Tamils.

**Deepavali:** Also known as the Festival of Lights, symbolising the conquest of good over evil, this is the most important festival in the Hindu calendar. Usually occurring in October or November, Little India is a hive of activity and turned into a fairyland setting of twinkling lights.

**Christmas:** Almost everyone, regardless of religious affiliation, gets into the spirit of exchanging gifts come Christmas time. Orchard Road is transformed into a riot of lights and glitzy displays, while shopping malls and hotels try to outdo each other with the most imaginative decorative displays. Christmas here has a definite Singaporean flavour.

**Hari Raya Puasa:** This Muslim celebration falls on the first day of the 10th Muslim month; the date varies from year to year. During Ramadan, the month preceding Hari Raya Puasa, all able Muslims observe a strict fast from sunrise to sunset. On Hari Raya Puasa, celebrants ask for forgiveness from family members, and feast on traditional food. Apart from the festival light-up at Geylang Serai, another hub of activity during the Muslim Hari Raya Puasa is to be found in the eclectic neighbourhood of Kampong Glam.

*City Hall*

# HERITAGE ARCHITECTURE

*There are some gems to discover in Singapore's heritage architecture, from the Civic District's grand and elegant colonial buildings and meticulously restored traditional shophouses, to iconic modern landmarks.*

Singapore's architecture showcases a spectrum of influences and styles from different periods. Over the past two decades, aggressive conservation efforts have been carried out to preserve Singapore's architectural heritage. This includes the restoration of historic buildings and adapting them for new uses. Examples are The Fullerton Hotel (formerly the General Post Office) and the National Art Gallery, which takes over the old Supreme Court building in 2015. Meanwhile, the Peranakan-style mould-ings and ornate decorations of shophouses can still be seen.

## SHOPHOUSES

Of all the architectural styles in Singapore, none is as distinctive as the lavishly decorated shophouses found in the city's older neighbourhoods. Known as Chinese Baroque or Singapore Eclectic architecture, these shophouses sport a rich mix of Malay, Chinese and European architectural details. The shophouse was so called because the lower floor was used for business while the upper level served as living quarters.

The design, initiated by Raffles, had detailed specifications to achieve conformity. They were arranged in a linear form and built of masonry with tile roofs. Linking the shophouses was a covered path called the 'five-foot way' because the width between the building and the street had to be exactly five feet. Over the years, five distinct shophouse styles developed, many of which have been restored to their original splendour.

The Early style was the first shophouses, erected in the 1840s. With their squat upper levels and simple lines, they

### Preserving Tiong Bahru

Unique pre-war architecture can be seen at the old housing estate of Tiong Bahru, about five minutes taxi ride from Outram and Chinatown. A 'Streamline Modern' architecture style with sweeping, aerodynamic lines is incorporated into some of these buildings and the designs are reminiscent of trains, ocean liners and aeroplanes. The post-war flats here are inspired by the International style. Today, Tiong Bahru's buildings are highly sought-after. A number of independent cafés have also set up shop here.

*Colourful shophouses*                    *Marina Bay Sands*

resemble dolls' houses. Dating back to the early 1900s, the First Transitional shophouses added an extra floor to maximise space. The Late style dating from 1910 to the late 1930s is the most florid of all shophouse styles, with lavishly decorated facades. The Second Transitional style from the late 1930s onwards combined Asian and European architectural influences, including Malay-style wooden eaves, Corinthian columns and pilasters and French windows with timber louvres. Art Deco is the most recent of styles, mainly built between 1940 and 1960. It is the most European in character; a private forecourt area with a gate and a balcony on the upper floor are typical features.

Many old shophouses are much sought-after these days because of their unique facades and historical value. Strict guidelines govern the restoration of shophouses, many of which have been turned into restaurants, bars and offices.

### COLONIAL BUILDINGS

Another collection of historic buildings are those built by the British during the colonial period. These structures generally feature Neo-classical, Palladian and Renaissance styles. Some of the most prominent examples include the Fullerton Building, the old Parliament House, the old Supreme Court Building, City Hall, the Victoria Theatre and Concert Hall, the National Museum of Singapore, Hill Street Central Fire Station, Raffles Hotel and Chijmes. Some of the city's main churches also feature the gothic style, including St Andrew's Cathedral and the Cathedral of the Good Shepherd, both of which are located in the City Hall district.

Aside from these grand structures, there are also charming 19th-century black and white bungalows in neighbourhoods such as Rochester, Tanglin Road, and Portsdown. Homes of top ranking government officials and the army during the colonial days, these were abandoned after the British left. Today, there are about 500 of these buildings left. Most have been renovated into beautiful residences and rented to expats, or leased to artists, architects and designers.

### MODERN ICONS

Singapore's skyline has changed dramatically over the past decade and today brims with gleaming skyscrapers and one-of-a-kind masterpieces. Iconic landmarks have popped up around town since the government introduced the two integrated resorts in 2010. Moshe Safdie's Marina Bay Sands, featuring three lofty towers crowned by a massive SkyPark and massive infinity pool, is the most talked about engineering wonder in the city. Other unique structures in the area include the white lotus-shaped Art Science museum and Gardens by the Bay's Flower Dome and Cloud Forest. Before these were built, Esplanade – Theatres on the Bay with its colossal dome-shaped structures was the highlight. It remains a significant landmark today.

*Singapore harbour in 1904*

# HISTORY: KEY DATES

*From a tiny fishing village to a pivotal trading post at the crossroads of the East and West, to the Asian economic powerhouse it is today, Singapore's evolution owes much to its inhabitants' ingenuity and hard work.*

## BRITISH COLONIAL RULE

| | |
|---|---|
| **1819** | Sir Stamford Raffles sets up a trading post for the British East India Company with the agreement of the Sultan of Johor and the Temenggong, his representative on the island. |
| **1824** | The Sultan cedes Singapore in perpetuity to the British. |
| **1826** | Singapore, with Malacca and Penang, becomes part of the Straits Settlements, under the control of British India. |
| **1867** | The Colonial Office in London takes over control of Singapore. |
| **1911** | The population of Singapore grows to 250,000 and the census records 48 races on the island, speaking 54 languages. It becomes the greatest naval base of the British empire east of Suez. |
| **1942** | The Japanese invade and occupy Singapore. |
| **1945** | The Japanese surrender and the Allied Forces return. |

## POST-WORLD WAR II

| | |
|---|---|
| **1946** | Singapore becomes a Crown Colony. |
| **1948** | The British allow limited elections to the Legislative Council. A state of emergency is declared in June, following the Malayan Communist Party's uprising against British imperialism. |
| **1955** | The Rendel Constitution granted by the British leads to general elections. |
| **1956** | People's Action Party (PAP) Central Executive Committee elections, in which the Communists decline to run, are held. Chinese students riot; PAP leaders are arrested. |
| **1958** | Singapore is granted partial independence. |
| **1959** | At the first general elections for a Legislative Assembly, PAP's Lee Kuan Yew becomes prime minister. |
| **1963** | Singapore joins the Federation of Malaysia. |

*British troops surrender to the Japanese in 1942*

| | |
|---|---|
| **1964** | PAP wins only one seat in the Malaysian general elections. Racial riots take place. |

## INDEPENDENCE

| | |
|---|---|
| **1965** | Singapore withdraws from the Federation and becomes a republic. It joins the United Nations and the Commonwealth. |
| **1967** | Singapore, Malaysia, Thailand, Indonesia and the Philippines form the Association of Southeast Asian Nations (ASEAN). |
| **1968** | In the first general elections, PAP wins all 58 seats. |
| **1987** | The US$5 billion Mass Rapid Transit (MRT) system opens. |
| **1990** | Lee Kuan Yew steps down after 31 years as prime minister and hands the reins over to Goh Chok Tong. The constitution is amended to provide for an elected president. |
| **1991** | PAP wins the elections, but loses four seats to the opposition. |
| **1993** | Ong Teng Cheong is Singapore's first elected president. |
| **1999** | S.R. Nathan of the minority Indian community is appointed president. |

## 21ST CENTURY

| | |
|---|---|
| **2002** | The landmark Esplanade – Theatres on the Bay opens. Al Qaeda-linked terrorist plot to bomb the US embassy uncovered. Some 15 suspects are arrested and jailed without trial. |
| **2003** | Outbreak of Severe Acute Respiratory Syndrome (SARS) in April. |
| **2004** | Lee Hsien Loong becomes Singapore's third prime minister. |
| **2008** | The Singapore Flyer, the world's tallest observation wheel, opens. The world's first Formula 1 night race is held in Singapore. |
| **2010** | Singapore's Integrated Resorts open. |
| **2012** | The sprawling Gardens by the Bay with its Super Trees and conservatories are unveiled. |
| **2015** | Singapore hosts the 2015 SEA games and ASEAN Paralympic games. The ruling People's Action Party (PAP) wins the general election with 69.9 percent of the vote. |
| **2017** | Halimah Yacob becomes Singapore's first female president. |
| **2018** | A historic meeting between the President of the United States, Donald Trump, and the Supreme Leader of North Korea, Kim Jong-un, takes place in Singapore. Singapore's most serious cyber-attack, targeting a health database, affects one and a half million people. |

# BEST ROUTES

*City Hall*

# CIVIC DISTRICT

*Many of the historical buildings in the Civic District have been restored and adapted for contemporary functions, but the genteel colonial elegance of the area remains unmistakable.*

---

**DISTANCE:** 2.5km (1.5 miles)
**TIME:** Half a day
**START:** St Andrew's Cathedral
**END:** Raffles Hotel
**POINTS TO NOTE:** Take the MRT to the City Hall station and turn left after the fare gates. This brings you to the side entrance of St Andrew's Cathedral. If you take a taxi, ask the driver to stop at the taxi stand at Raffles City Shopping Centre and then cross the road to the church.

---

In his town plan of 1822, Stamford Raffles designated the area north of the Singapore River as the colonial hub, ordering the building of offices, banks, hotels, churches and clubs. The area, roughly between the City Hall and Dhoby Ghaut MRT stations, is now known as the Civic District.

## ST ANDREW'S CATHEDRAL

Grab a bite at **Tiong Bahru Bakery**, see ❶, in Raffles City. This I.M. Pei-designed complex comprises a shopping mall, the 72-storey Swissôtel the Stamford and the 26-storey Fairmont Singapore. Beneath the complex is the City Hall MRT station, which is linked via the subterranean CityLink Mall to Suntec City and the Esplanade – Theatres on the Bay.

After having your coffee fix, start your journey at the graceful **St Andrew's Cathedral** ❶ (http://cathedral.org.sg; Mon–Sat 9am–4.30pm, Sun 7am–5pm). This English Gothic-style church was built by Indian convict labourers, who used a special plaster known as Madras *chunam*, made of egg white, egg shells, lime, sugar and coconut husk, to achieve the gleaming white exterior. The structure you see today is actually the second church to have been built on this site, designed by Ronald MacPherson and consecrated in 1862. The earlier Palladian-style building was struck by lightning twice and demolished in 1852.

Architecturally significant and steeped in history, the cathedral has, befittingly, been declared a national monument. Note the pretty stained-glass windows behind the altar. Known as the East Windows, the three panels are dedicated

*St Andrew's Cathedral*

to Stamford Raffles, John Crawfurd, the second resident of Singapore, and Major General William Butterworth, a governor of the Straits Settlement. Behind the pulpit is the Coventry Cross, formed by nails salvaged from the ruins of England's Coventry Cathedral, which was destroyed during World War II.

## THE PADANG

A diagonal path leads from the cathedral to the green expanse known as the **Padang** ❷ ('field' in Malay), along St Andrew's Road. Known as the Esplanade in colonial times, this was where the Europeans played cricket and socialised in the cool of the evenings. In 1942, during the Japanese Occupation, European civilians were rounded up on the Padang and forced to march 22km (14 miles) to Changi, where they were imprisoned. Today the Padang plays host to public events and rugby and cricket matches.

On either side of the Padang are private clubs, the venerable Victorian-style **Singapore Cricket Club** to your right and the newer **Singapore Recreation Club** to your left.

## CITY HALL

Across St Andrew's Road from the Padang are two handsome structures that were once Singapore's most important government buildings. In 1945 Lord Louis Mountbatten

### Map labels

National Museum
Cathedral of the Good Shepherd ❶❺
Mint Museum of Toys
Stamford Road
Fort Canning Tunnel
Stamford Street
Victoria Street
Bras Basah Road
North Bridge Rd
Cashin St
Raffles Hotel ❶❼
Chijmes ❶❻
Fairmont Singapore
Peranakan Museum
Loke Yew St
Armenian Street
Stamford House
Stamford Court
Raffles City
Canning Rise
National Archives
Capitol Theatre
Armenian Church of St Greogry the Illuminator ❶❹
City Hall Road
Swissôtel The Stamford
Singapore Philatelic Museum
Coleman Street
St Andrew's Cathedral ❶
WAR MEMORIAL PARK
Central Fire Station ❶❸
North Bridge Road
Singapore Recreation Club
MICA Building ❶❷
High Street
City Hall
New Supreme Court ❸
Supreme Court Lane
PADANG ❷
St Andrew's Rd
Connaught Drive
Hill Street
Coleman Bridge
North Bridge Road
Parliament
Old Supreme Court ❹ ❺
National Gallery Singapore
Cenotaph
Elgin Bridge
North Boat Quay
Parliament House
Parliament Court
The Arts House ❶❶
Singapore Cricket Club
ESPLANADE PARK
Victoria Theatre and Concert Hall ❻
Parliament Lane
Esplanade Bridge
South Bridge Road
Raffles' Landing Site ❾
Sir Stamford Raffles Statue
Asian Civilisation Museum ❽
Esplanade Drive
South Boat Quay
Singapore
Anderson Bridge
Cavenagh Bridge
One Fullerton
Raffles Place
200 m / 220 yds

*National Gallery Singapore*

accepted the Japanese surrender on the grand staircase of the **City Hall ❸**, which was completed in 1929. It was also here, in front of the grand Grecian columns, that Lee Kuan Yew declared Singapore's self-government status in 1959 and the country's independence in 1963.

*Court buildings*

Next to the City Hall is the green-domed **Old Supreme Court ❹**, built in 1939. Of note is the tympanum sculpture by Italian sculptor Cavalieri Rudolfo Nolli. He is said to have used his daughter as his model for the centre figure of Justice, which is flanked by figures representing a lost soul, the law, gratitude, prosperity and abundance.

The Old Supreme Court and City Hall buildings have been skilfully converted into the **National Gallery Singapore** (www.nationalgallery.sg; Sat–Thu 10am–7pm, Fri 10am–9pm). Ten years in the making, the gallery was opened in 2015 to mark the nation's 50th anniversary of independence. Its thought-provoking exhibitions make use of the vast 8,000-plus piece collection – making this the largest public collection of modern art in Singapore and Southeast Asia.

Looming right behind the National Gallery Singapore is the glass-and-steel **New Supreme Court ❺**, capped by a futuristic disc. The observation deck on the 8th floor (free) offers excellent views of the city.

### VICTORIA THEATRE AND CONCERT HALL

Cross Parliament Place and continue past the Old Parliament House to the **Victoria Theatre** and **Victoria Concert Hall ❻** (www.vtvch.com), which are linked by a landmark clock tower. Although the two neoclassical buildings were designed to match, the theatre – completed in 1862 as a town hall – predates the 1902 concert hall, although both have received major facelifts in recent years. Since 1979, Victoria Concert Hall – an important performing space for theatre, dance and music – has been home to the Singapore Symphony Orchestra.

For the centenary of Singapore's founding in 1919, a bronze **statue of Sir Stamford Raffles ❼**, cast by T. Woolner, was relocated from the Padang to the Victoria Memorial Hall, now the Victoria Concert Hall. It was moved to

---

## Mint Museum of Toys

Across from the Raffles Hotel, on Seah Street, is the Mint Museum of Toys (tel: 6339 0660; www.emint.com; daily 9.30am–6.30pm), a trove of rare toys, from vintage Popeye the Sailor and Felix the Cat to superheroes like Batman and Superman, put together by Chang Ya Fa, who started his collection when he was just six years old. To date he has accumulated some 50,000 pieces, estimated to be worth S$5 million, from auctions and curio shops around the world.

*The Chamber in The Arts House.*

the National Museum during World War II and thereafter returned to the forecourt of the concert hall in 1946.

## ASIAN CIVILISATIONS MUSEUM

From the theatre and concert hall, move on to the **Asian Civilisations Museum** ❽ (www.acm.org.sg; Sat–Thu 10am–7pm, Fri 10am–9pm) on Empress Place. The original building was completed in 1865 and designed in Neoclassical style by J.F. McNair. Be sure to devote enough time to this wonderful museum, which has 11 galleries. Its diverse collection of artefacts, from prehistoric agricultural tools to textiles and bronzeware, reveal Asia's cultural and historical complexities.

In the China Gallery, displays such as Chinese deities and fragile Dehua porcelain are the highlights, while the Koran-inspired calligraphic art in the West Asia Gallery is impressive. The South Asia galleries hold religious statuary and architectural motifs of the Indian subcontinent.

## RAFFLES' LANDING SITE

Continue on the leafy promenade by the Singapore River to the **Raffles' Landing Site** ❾. Here stands another statue of Stamford Raffles, a white marble replica of the original in front of the Victoria Concert Hall, which marks the spot on the northern bank where Raffles first stepped ashore on 28 January 1819. There are fine views of Boat Quay and the Central Business District across the river.

## THE ARTS HOUSE

Adjacent to the Raffles' Landing Site is **The Arts House** ❿ (www.theartshouse. sg; daily 10am–10pm; free), a multidisciplinary arts centre occupying the former Parliament House, which was built in 1827. The building was originally designed to be the private residence of a wealthy merchant. It was instead used as the first Court House and Assembly House, and then by the Parliament until 1999. In its grounds is a bronze elephant statue, a gift from King Chulalongkorn of Siam in 1871. The Arts House has a busy schedule of film screenings, art exhibitions, and theatre and dance performances. Its 200-seat performance space, named the Chamber, was where members of parliament debated bills and laws in the past. Today they exchange views in the austere **Parliament House** ⓫ located just behind the Arts House.

## MICA BUILDING

If you decide to call it a day, cross Cavenagh Bridge to the Raffles Place MRT station. If you are keen to explore the Civic District further, then walk by the riverside to Elgin Bridge; on its right is an underpass that takes you to North Boat Quay. Cross the road to Hill Street, site of the **MICA Building** ⓬, the Renaissance-style headquarters of the Ministry of Information, Communications and the Arts. The building, erected in 1934 with 911 technicoloured window shutters, used to be

*The Civil Defence Heritage Gallery*

the Old Hill Street Police Station. On its ground floor is the **ARtrium**, with several art galleries showcasing the works of local and Asian artists.

Turn left as you exit the MICA Building and walk along Hill Street. Next to the building is a steep staircase, which leads up to **Fort Canning Park** (see page 38).

## CENTRAL FIRE STATION

Further along is the **Central Fire Station** ⑬, the oldest fire station in Singapore, housed in a fine example of the 'Blood and Bandage' architectural style, completed in 1901. This style, with alternating exposed brickwork and whitewashed plaster, is a departure from the usual Palladian and classical styles prevailing in Singapore at the time.

The fire station also houses the **Civil Defence Heritage Gallery** (www.scdf. gov.sg; Tue–Sun 10am–5pm; free), a unique museum with displays of antique fire engines and interactive stations depicting firefighting operations. On the guided tour, you get to climb up the hose tower, the lookout point in the early days.

## ARMENIAN CHURCH

Across Coleman Street from the fire station is the **Armenian Church of St Gregory the Illuminator** ⑭ (http://armeniansinasia.org; daily 10am–6pm), the oldest church in Singapore, built in 1835. This is where Singapore's small Armenian community congregates on

Sunday. The tombstones of prominent Armenians in Singapore's history lie in its memorial garden. Among them are the tombstones of the Sarkies brothers who founded the Raffles Hotel, and Agnes Joaquim, who discovered the orchid hybrid *Vanda Miss Joaquim*, now Singapore's national flower.

## CATHEDRAL OF THE GOOD SHEPHERD

At the intersection of Victoria Street and Bras Basah Road on the left is the **Cathedral of the Good Shepherd** ⑮ (https://cathedral.catholic.sg; Mon–Fri 7am–9pm, Sat–Sun 8am–9pm), the oldest Roman Catholic church in Singapore and a national monument. Completed in 1846, it was designed by Denis Lesley Sweeney. Its architecture recalls that of England's St Martin-in-the-Fields and St Paul's in Covent Garden, while the three bells in the steeple were cast by the Auguste Hildebrand Foundry in Paris. In its grounds is the residence of the current Archbishop of Singapore, a simple two-storey bungalow with a portico and enclosed verandahs.

## CHIJMES

Opposite the cathedral across Victoria Street is the restaurant and entertainment hub **Chijmes** ⑯ (www.chijmes. com.sg), pronounced 'chimes'. The Gothic-style buildings were formerly occupied by the Convent of the Holy Infant Jesus,

*The Mint Museum of Toys*          *The historic complex of Chijmes*

founded in 1854. The Sisters on the Seine from France ran a school with boarding facilities for girls and an orphanage.

The conversion of a convent school and religious building into a nightlife hub did not take place without controversy, but it is generally agreed that the restoration was tastefully done; the mouldings in the chapel and along the walkway are especially beautiful, and the fountain courtyard is a pleasant place for a break. Peek into the old chapel, which has exquisite stained glass. Speciality shops and restaurants line the cloistered walkways. A good place for lunch here is **Lei Garden**, see ❷.

## RAFFLES HOTEL

Exit Chijmes at the intersection of Bras Basah and North Bridge roads. Diagonally opposite Chijmes is the last stop of your tour, the legendary **Raffles Hotel** ⓱ (www.raffles.com). Built in 1887 by the Sarkies brothers and restored in the 1990s (and more recently in 2018–19), the hotel has welcomed numerous famous personalities over the years. Somerset Maugham summed up its spirit best when he wrote that the 'Raffles stands for all the fables of the exotic East'. The genteel air of this national monument is still palpable today and is best soaked up in the leafy courtyard with its antique fountains. The **shopping arcade** has bespoke tailors, antiques stores and luxury boutiques showcasing brands like Tiffany & Co., Coach and Louis Vuitton.

At the time of writing the hotel was still undergoing renovation, due to reopen in the first half of 2019. Works will see the addition of a new lobby area, upgraded suites, a new spa in Raffles Arcade and an expanded pool and fitness area. The famous Jubilee Hall will be reborn as the **Jubilee Ballroom**, with room for 300 guests, while you'll find a refreshed selection of bars and restaurants for eveningtime diversions. The noted **Long Bar** – which has remained open at a pop-up location during the renovation – is where you can try the famous Singapore Sling, first created as a lady's cocktail in 1910 by Chinese bartender Ngiam Tong Boon.

If you're here after the renovation, dine at one of Raffles's revitalised restaurants.

## Food and drink

### ❶ TIONG BAHRU BAKERY
B1-11/12 Raffles City Shopping Centre; tel: 6333 4160; www.tiongbahrubakery. com; daily 8am–10pm; $$
This popular outlet, a partnership between Gontran Cherrier, Parisian celebrity baker, and Singapore's Spa Esprit Group, serves French-style baked goods with a twist.

### ❷ LEI GARDEN
01-24 Chijmes; tel: 6339 3822; daily 11.30am–3pm, 6–10.30pm; $$$
This venerable Chinese restaurant serves well-executed dim sum alongside fresh seafood, barbecue pork and roast duck.

*Waxwork exhibit at The BattleBox*

# MUSEUM DISTRICT

*Tiny Singapore has a disproportionately large number of museums, located all over the island. Thankfully for visitors, the major ones, such as the National Museum, Peranakan Museum and Singapore Art Museum, are conveniently clustered in the Civic District in a zone known as the Museum District.*

**DISTANCE:** Varies, depending on the number of museums visited
**TIME:** A full day
**START:** Raffles City
**END:** Singapore Art Museum
**POINTS TO NOTE:** Take the MRT to the City Hall station and head to the Raffles City Shopping Centre for breakfast.

Among Singapore's many museums, there are historical ones that catalogue the island's early stories through artefacts and war relics; art and design museums that showcase cutting-edge creativity; and quirky repositories that display unique tastes. This route brings you to four museums, each offering different insights into the city's heritage.

A good breakfast option in the area is **Cedele**, see ①, in Raffles City. After breakfast, exit the mall and walk down Stamford Road, past the resplendent **Stamford House**.

Turn left onto Hill Street, pass the Armenian Church and turn right onto Canning Rise, which brings you to **Fort Canning Park**.

## FORT CANNING PARK

Explore **Fort Canning Park** ① on its well-marked paths. History abounds on Fort Canning Hill, once known as Bukit Larangan (Forbidden Hill) as commoners were not allowed here. Archaeological excavations indicate that the Malay princes who ruled Singapore in the 14th century had their palaces here. Stamford Raffles also built his residence here in 1823, as the hill afforded an excellent vantage point for keeping watch on Singapore's coastline. In 1860 the British built a fort, from which cannon fire announced dawn, noon and dusk daily.

The hill also holds an old tomb said to contain the remains of Iskandar Shah, the last ruler of pre-colonial Singapore. This has been consecrated as a Muslim *keramat* (shrine).

Behind the whitewashed Fort Canning Centre is **The BattleBox** (http://www.battlebox.com.sg; daily 9.30am–5.30pm, entry via guided tour only), which reo-

*Peranakan Museum*

pened in 2016 following a two-year renovation. The bunker, with its maze-like complex of rooms and corridors 9m (30ft) underground, was constructed in 1936 as the nerve centre of British military operations in Southeast Asia. Today, it's a museum chronicling the fall of Singapore to the Japanese during World War II through exhibitions featuring videos, artefacts, documents and wax-work tableaux; tours last around an hour and a quarter and guides are professional and knowledgeable. It was here on 15 February 1942 that British officers made the decision to surrender. Adjacent to The Battle-Box is a 1926 building that served as an army barracks; it now houses Hotel Fort Canning and The Legends Fort Canning Park country club.

Walk down the patch of green known as Fort Canning Green, which used to be an old Christian cemetery until 1865, towards the entrance that is marked by two Gothic gates. Leave the park and walk down Canning Rise towards Coleman Street, past the Registry of Marriages. On your right is **The Singapore Philatelic Museum ❷** (23B Coleman Street; www.spm.org.sg; daily 10am–7pm), which offers a unique

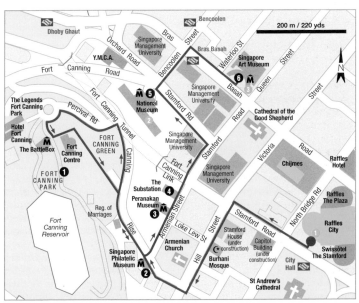

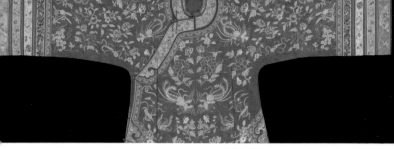

*Silk bridal gown at the Peranakan Musuem*

window into Singapore's history. It has displays of postcards, first-day covers and stamps from the private collections of renowned philatelists.

### PERANAKAN MUSEUM

After visiting the stamp museum, turn into Armenian Street where the **Peranakan Museum** ❸ (www.peranakanmuseum. org.sg; daily 10am–7pm, Fri until 9pm) is located. The building that houses the Peranakan Museum was formerly occupied by the Tao Nan School. Set up by Hokkien immigrants to preserve their cultural heritage, it was the first school in Singa-pore to use Mandarin as the medium of instruction.

This museum was the first in the world dedicated to Peranakan heritage and material culture. Peranakans, or Straits Chinese, have a fascinating hybrid culture that has evolved since the 17th century and years of intermarriage between immigrant Chinese men and local Malay women in the former British Straits Settlements of Singapore, Malacca and Penang.

Peranakan life and heritage are thematically presented in 10 permanent galleries. Themes include the origins of the Peranakans, the fastidious 12-day Peranakan wedding, the role of the Nonya, the Peranakan woman, as well as Peranakan cuisine, which occupies pride of place within Peranakan culture.

Two notable exhibits are located in the **Wedding Gallery**. A 19th-century silk bridal gown, adorned with embroidered phoenixes and peonies, is typical of that worn by Peranakan brides in Singapore and Malacca. Another major exhibit is the wedding bed, ornately carved with auspicious motifs and decorated with embroidered hangings and beads. The wedding bed is traditionally one of the largest pieces of furniture in the homes of wealthy Peranakans.

The **Food and Feasting Gallery** presents glimpses into Peranakan cuisine and dining customs. Elaborately set up here is a *tok panjang* (long table), laden with colourful porcelain of all shapes and sizes, used for the traditional

### Peranakans

Peranakan men are known as *baba* and the women as *nonya*. They were the first locals to speak English and adopt Western customs during the colonial times. In fact, their loyalty to the British led some to describe them as the 'King's Chinese'. They speak a Chinese-Malay patois, and their culture is derived from the traditions of these ethnic groups. Most perceptibly, Peranakan culinary heritage is a blend of Malay and Chinese cooking styles and ingredients. Many Peranakan families used to reside in Emerald Hill and Katong, in terrace houses that sport a distinctive architectural style. Having intermarried with other ethnic groups, Peranakans have become less distinct as a racial group.

*Historical photographs at the National Museum*

12-course feast held during weddings and special occasions.

## THE SUBSTATION

Leave the museum and walk down Armenian Street. At no. 45 is **The Substation** ❹ (www.substation.org; Mon–Thu 10am–7pm, Fri noon–7pm), an independent arts centre converted from a disused power station. Its small theatre is often the stage for experimental drama and dance productions. Peep into the gallery; you may stumble upon the exhibition of an emerging visual artist. In the garden of The Substation, you will find Timbre Music Bistro (www.timbre.com.sg; daily 6pm–1am, Fri–Sat until 2am), a popular live-music venue with great pub grub and local musicians performing nightly.

## NATIONAL MUSEUM

At the end of Armenian Street, cross the road to Stamford Road and turn left after the Singapore Management University's School of Accountancy on your left. Further ahead on the left is the **National Museum** ❺ (www.national museum.sg; daily 10am–7pm; free entry to some permanent galleries). Before you tour the museum, stop for lunch at **Flutes**, see ❶.

Opened in 1887, the original building was designed by J.F. McNair as the former Raffles Library and Museum. Designed in elegant neo-Palladian style, the building was expanded in 1906,

1914 and 1916. The museum emerged from another major facelift, the most extensive reconstruction and conservation project in its history, in late 2006.

The building, restored to its former splendour, has a modern glass-and-steel wing, whose star attraction is the beautiful **Glass Rotunda**. Designed as a modern interpretation of the original **Rotunda Dome**, the glass rotunda lights up like a lantern at night, with projected images that depict Singapore's history.

For the original Rotunda Dome's restoration, experts took down its curved stained-glass panels, which were then restored by a professional stained-glass artist who used 18th-century reinforcement techniques. The Victorian floral and square patterns remain as vivid as ever, particularly following the buffing and cleaning of the stained-glass pieces. Go up on the four-storey **Glass Passage** to view the dome's exterior architectural details such as the elegant Palladian motifs and 19th-century fish-scale zinc tiles.

*Galleries*

There are two main sections in the National Museum: the **History Gallery** and four **Living Galleries**. The history section traces Singapore's past from the 14th century to the present day through two complementary 'paths' that chronicle key events and the everyday experiences of citizens.

The Living Galleries afford insights into everyday life in modern-day Singapore through its engaging fashion, film, food

*Displays in Singapore National Museum*

and photography sections. In the **Food Gallery**, for example, you can find out more about Singapore's street food from the 1950s to 1970s: Not only do you see and 'hear' the installations, you can also catch whiffs of the different types of food and spices.

The **Exhibition Galleries** are where temporary exhibits are staged. A prominent past exhibition featured 130 classical Greek and Hellenistic artefacts from the Louvre in Paris.

### National Treasures

Don't forget to look out for the 10 'National Treasures' – historically significant and rare artefacts selected from the National Museum's collection, which date from the 14th century to the mid-20th century.

One important relic of the country's pre-colonial history is the **Singapore Stone**, located in the Singapore History Gallery. It is engraved with the earliest inscription found on the island. What you can see in the museum is the remains of a large boulder that originally stood by the Singapore River, near where the Fullerton Hotel stands today. The boulder split into three parts after it was blown up in the 19th century for the widening of the river. The full inscription, dating from the 10th to the 14th century, has not been deciphered as scholars cannot agree either the date of origin or the language, thought to be a variant of an old Sumatran script.

Another highlight in the History Gallery is the 19th-century **will of Munshi Abdullah**, who is known as the Father of modern Malay literature. A contemporary of Stamford Raffles and Colonel William Farquhar, he is most well known for his magnum opus *Hikayat Abdullah (The Story of Abdullah)*, which contains his first-hand impressions of the island after 1819, the year Sultan Hussein of Johor allowed the British East India Company to establish a trading post in Singapore. Munshi's will, dating to 1854, is a rare document, as wills were uncommon during his time.

The museum has an excellent Chinese puppetry collection, of which the **Xin Sai Le Puppet Stage**, found in the Film and Wayang Gallery, is another interesting National Treasure. Chinese puppet shows were a popular form of street entertainment for immigrants from the 19th to the early 20th century. This glove-puppet theatre stage, with its 1,000 light bulbs, belonged to the Xin Sai Le troupe from the Fujian province in South China, which visited Singapore in the 1930s. The whole theatre could be dismantled or assembled within an hour by the troupe. The collection features 45 puppets, 96 costumes, 56 hats, 24 pieces of backdrops, accessories and 20 pieces of props, stored in two wooden chests.

## SINGAPORE ART MUSEUM

From the National Museum, cross Stamford Road to Bencoolen Street, walk past the buildings of the Singapore Management University and turn right. Further along on Bras Basah Road is

*Contemporary art in the Singapore Art Museum*

the **Singapore Art Museum** ❻ (www. singaporeartmuseum.sg; daily 10am–7pm, Fri until 9pm).

### Historical building

Hailed as a national monument, the 1855 museum building once housed St Joseph's Institution, a Catholic boys' school founded in 1852 and run by the La Salle Brothers. After 135 years on Bras Basah Road, the school was relocated in 1987 and the building was sensitively restored as Singapore's national art museum. Note the former chapel, now the museum's auditorium, featuring a stained-glass installation by Filipino contemporary artist Ramon Orlina. Original architectural features that have been retained include the pretty courtyards, shuttered windows and ceramic floor tiles.

### Collection

Institutional and private collectors in Singapore avidly amass art from the region, and this museum houses one of the most impressive collections. It has an excellent sampling of works by leading Asian artists, such as Affandi and Hendra Gunawan from Indonesia and Chinese Nobel Prize laureate Gao Xingjian.

The museum also holds Singapore's national art collection. The permanent collection of over 7,500 artworks includes representative works of well-known local artists such as Liu Kang and Georgette Chen. One particular highlight is Chen's *Still Life with Orange and Apples*. The museum has acquired 94 of her paintings, which comprise portraits, still lifes and landscapes.

The museum's **Trattoria Lafiandra**, see ❸, is a great option for refuelling.

## Food and drink

### ❶ CEDELE BAKERY CAFE
03-28A Raffles City Shopping Centre; tel: 6334 4828; www.cedelegroup.com; Mon–Thu 8am–9.30pm, Fri 8am–10pm, Sat 9am–10pm, Sun 9am–9.30pm; $$
This outlet of a home-grown bakery chain serves a great all-day breakfast. Fill up with the hearty Big Breakfast Set with bacon, sausages, scrambled eggs and mushrooms.

### ❷ FLUTES
The National Museum of Singapore, 93 Stamford Road; tel: 6338 8770; www. flutes.com.sg; Mon–Fri 11.30am–2pm and 6.30–10pm, Sat 6.30–10.30pm, weekend brunch 10.30am–2.30pm (4pm on Sun), afternoon tea for parties of 10+; $$$$
Dine on modern European flavours and pair the dishes with wines from the extensive drinks list.

### ❸ TRATTORIA LAFIANDRA
Singapore Art Museum; tel: 6884 4035; www.lafiandra.com.sg; daily noon–3pm and 6–11pm; $$
A quaint Italian trattoria offering an impressive choice of antipasti, homemade pasta dishes and main courses.

# MARINA BAY

*Singapore's newer iconic structures such as the Marina Bay Sands, the Esplanade Theatres, the Singapore Flyer and the Marina Bay Financial Centre dominate the ever-changing Marina Bay district.*

**DISTANCE:** 3km
**TIME:** Full day
**START:** Esplanade
**END:** Helix Bridge
**POINTS TO NOTE:** Take the MRT to the City Hall station and turn right into CityLink Mall after the fare gates. Follow the signs to Esplanade. From there, you can explore the entire Marina Bay loop.

The Singapore River empties into the Marina Bay, an artificial inlet formed by reclaimed land. Marina Bay is also the name of the area around the bay, the city's new downtown. A landscaped promenade forms a continuous pedestrian route along the waterfront, linking the Esplanade to Collyer Quay and the Marina Bay Sands Integrated Resort.

## THE ESPLANADE

Start your tour at **The Esplanade – Theatres on the Bay ❶**. The S$600 million Esplanade (www.esplanade.com) was somewhat controversial when it was com-

pleted in 2002, with the spiny exterior of its two colossal dome-shaped auditoriums often compared to the thorny husks of the durian fruit. Singaporeans have, however, grown to love this bold architectural statement.

Try to catch a performance in the Esplanade's 1,600-seat concert hall or 2,000-seat theatre, both of which have outstanding acoustics. The well-regarded **Singapore Symphony Orchestra** performs its season at the concert hall (box office open daily noon–8.30pm).

After your Esplanade tour, have an early lunch at **No Signboard Seafood**, see ❶, at the Esplanade Mall. If you return for an evening performance, try **Makansutra Gluttons Bay** outside the mall.

## ESPLANADE PARK

From the shopping centre, exit onto the **Marina Bay Promenade**. Walk along the waterfront; the view of the CBD skyline from here is fantastic. Continue under the **Esplanade Bridge** to the **Esplanade Park ❷**, a green belt along Connaught Drive.

*Singapore's skyline, including Marina Bay, in the morning light*

At the park's northern end is the Victorian-style **Tan Kim Seng Fountain**, constructed to mark the merchant's contribution in 1857 to the building of the town's water works. The **Cenotaph**, whose granite surface is engraved with the words 'Our Glorious Dead', is dedicated to the 124 British men who lost their lives in World War I. After World War II, more inscriptions were added. At the southern end is the **Lim Bo Seng Memorial**, dedicated to the war hero who led the anti-Japanese resistance movement, Force 136, in World War II.

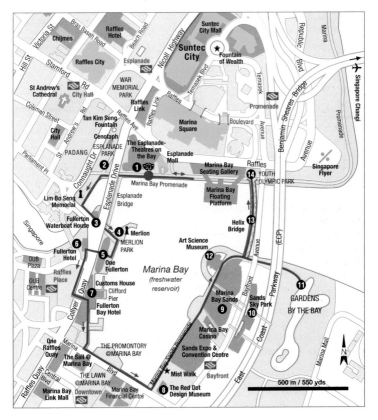

*Merlion Park*

Make your way to the pedestrian path along Anderson Bridge. Ahead is the Art Deco-style **Fullerton Waterboat House ❸** (1919), which once supplied water to ships at sea. Restored with its original curved facade intact, the building now houses a rooftop bar and restaurant.

## MERLION PARK

Just before the Waterboat House, turn left and follow the path to the **Merlion Park ❹**. By the water's edge is an 8.6m (28ft) -high statue of the water-spewing Merlion. First unveiled in 1964, the iconic landmark has a lion's head, which recalls the myth of ancient Singapore's founder Sang Nila Utama, said to have spotted a lion on the island around the 14th century. Its fish tail symbolises the city's modest beginnings as a fishing village.

## FULLERTON BUILDINGS

Next to the Merlion Park is the glass-and-steel **One Fullerton ❺**, with a clutch of restaurants and cafés offering alfresco, waterfront seating.

## Singapore Flyer

The 165m (540ft) -high Singapore Flyer (www.singaporeflyer.com; daily 8.30am–10.30pm) is an observation wheel offering panoramic views of Malaysian and Indonesian islands as well as Singapore's city skyline.

The **Fullerton Hotel ❻** is linked by an underpass to One Fullerton. It occupies a 1924 building named after Robert Fullerton, the first governor of the Straits Settlements, and is a fine example of the Edwardian Baroque neoclassical style. Before it was restored and reopened as a hotel in 2001, the building was the Chamber of Commerce and General Post Office.

## COLLYER QUAY

The Fullerton Waterboat House, Fullerton Hotel and One Fullerton make up a leisure precinct known as **Fullerton Heritage**, which also comprises the **Collyer Quay** area, further south along the waterfront. The re-developed **Customs House ❼** today houses The Fullerton Bay Hotel, several restaurants and bars with stunning views of the bay. From the Customs House, walk along the waterfront promenade to the Red Dot Design Museum.

## RED DOT DESIGN MUSEUM

Run by the German body that presents the prestigious Red Dot Award, the **Red Dot Design Museum ❽** (www.museum.red-dot.sg; Mon–Thu 10am–8pm, Fri–Sun 10am–11pm) moved to its present site on Marina Blvd in late 2017. The cutting-edge glass-fronted museum showcases slick product design from around the world. The design shop is high quality, and its café and bar are fittingly stylish. Continue along the promenade which links to **Marina Bay Sands**.

*Fullerton Hotel*                    *Supertree Grove at Gardens by the Bay*

## MARINA BAY SANDS

The centrepiece of this area is the massive **Marina Bay Sands** ❾ (www.marinabaysands.com) – the most expensive development ever built by the American casino-resort giant, Las Vegas Sands. This 'integrated resort' has transformed Singapore's skyline since it was completed in 2010; the mega leisure, entertainment and hospitality complex features a casino, luxury hotel, convention facilities, high-end boutiques, a theatre, nightclubs, bars and restaurants.

One of the many 'engineering wonders' here is the 200m **Sands Sky Park** ❿ (Mon–Thu 9.30am–10pm, Fri–Sun 9.30am–11pm), a fascinating structure designed by architect Moshe Safdie. Perched on top of the three lofty hotel towers are a sweeping 1.2-hectare tropical park with landscaped gardens, an observation deck, and an infinity pool with amazing views of the skyline.

To the west of Marina Bay Sands Integrated Resort is the **Marina Bay Financial Centre**, an extension of the CBD.

## GARDENS BY THE BAY

Across the highway via a pedestrian bridge is an area called **Gardens by the Bay** ⓫ (daily 5am–2am outdoor gardens, 9am–9pm conservatories and OCBC Skyway) featuring two lush conservatories: the Flower Dome, with a controlled 22°C environment, and the Cloud Forest, which boasts the world's tallest indoor waterfall.

There are also a dozen towering Supertrees offering shade in the day and a glittering light display at night. Two of the Supertrees are connected by the OCBC Skyway, with views of the sprawling area.

Adjacent to Marina Bay Sands complex is the **Art Science Museum** ⓬ (daily 10am–7pm). The white lotus-shaped building houses galleries exhibiting art, science, media, design and architecture.

Another engineering masterpiece nearby is the world's first **double helix curved bridge** ⓭ which allows pedestrians to walk across from Marina Bay Sands to the other side of the waterfront where luxury hotels like the Ritz-Carlton Millenia and the Mandarin Oriental are located. This bridge affords top views of beautiful sunsets and of the bay itself from its look-out points. You can end your tour at the **Youth Olympic Park** ⓮, an 'art park' with creative installations by local youth. It is right at the end of the Helix Bridge and near the Floating Stadium. Alternatively, walk over to the foot of the Singapore Flyer and enjoy a meal at the 1960s-themed food street.

## Food and drink

**❶ NO SIGNBOARD SEAFOOD**
01-14/16 Esplanade Mall; tel: 6336 9959; www.nosignboardseafood.com; daily 11am–10.30pm; $$
This well-established restaurant serves a range of fresh seafood creations.

# SINGAPORE RIVER

*The Singapore River is where the city's modern history began. Take a trip along the river to marvel at colonial-era bridges, stately buildings and conservation shophouses that reflect the city's past.*

**DISTANCE:** 1.5km (1 mile)
**TIME:** 3–4 hours
**START:** Merlion Park
**END:** Clarke Quay or Merlion Park
**POINTS TO NOTE:** Walk from the Raffles Place MRT station to the Merlion Park, or take a taxi to One Fullerton, which is next to the park. This is recommended as an afternoon-to-evening tour. You can combine this tour with route 3 (see page 44).

Spanning almost 4km (2.5 miles) from its mouth at Marina Bay to Kim Seng Bridge on the other end, the Singapore River was the island's commercial lifeline for more than a century, where Stamford Raffles and other early immigrants first landed. The swamps and grisly floating skulls deposited by pirates are now long gone, as are the labourers and junks, and its quays are lined by colourful conservation shophouses and warehouses.

### River cruise

A leisurely way to enjoy the sights along the banks is to board the **Singapore River Experience** (www.rivercruise.com.sg), a pleasant 30-minute cruise on an environmentally friendly electric bumboat, designed to look like a traditional one of yesteryear. Purchase your ticket (daily 9am–10.30pm) at the Singapore River Cruises & Leisure booth at the jetty at the **Merlion Park ❶**. The boat wends its way from Marina Bay (see page 44) to Boat Quay and Clarke Quay, passing under several bridges, and then turns around at the Liang Court jetty for the return journey to the Merlion Park. If you have more time, you can also opt for the 45-minute cruise further upriver to Robertson Quay.

However, if you prefer to alight at any point along the river, such as at Clarke Quay as recommended in this route, purchase a one-way river taxi ticket. The operator of the Singapore River Experience cruise runs a river taxi service that will take you from one point to another along the Singapore River.

*The curve of Boat Quay represents the belly of the carp, an auspicious shape*

Rates depend on destinations. Let the attendants know in advance where you want to disembark. Buy your ticket and board at any of the nine jetties along the Singapore River.

## HISTORICAL BRIDGES

When you board the boat, be sure to take advantage of the good photo opportunities of buildings like The Esplanade – Theatres on the Bay (see page 44) and Fullerton Hotel (see page 44).

The Singapore River flows under 12 bridges, many of which are historical structures with beautiful designs. The cruise takes you under the first bridge, **Anderson Bridge ❷**, built in 1910 to link the colonial district (now the Civic District) and the commercial district (present-day Raffles Place).

You then pass under **Cavenagh Bridge ❸**. Made in Scotland and reassembled in Singapore, the bridge was named after Major-General Orfeur Cavenagh, Governor of the Straits Settlement from 1859 to 1867. It was originally planned as a drawbridge but upon completion was found to be appropriate only as a fixed structure. Now it serves as a pedestrian bridge linking the north and south banks.

## BOAT QUAY

As the cruise continues, to your left is **Boat Quay ❹**, which runs along the south bank between Cavenagh Bridge and Elgin Bridge. Boat Quay was a trading hub from the colonial days until the 1970s, when lighters were banned from the river, and flotsam and jetsam was cleared. Its shophouses, which held cargo in the early days, were restored to their former glory and updated as restaurants and bars.

Today's Boat Quay has seen better days, having been eclipsed by the revitalised Clarke Quay (see below). Nevertheless, its eclectic mix of alfresco

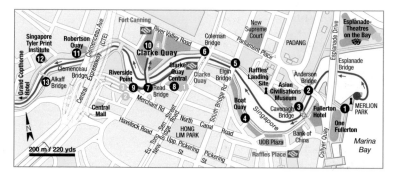

*Nightlife at Clarke Quay*

eateries, lively Irish pubs and trendy bars still appeals to executives from the vicinity and tourists seeking to dine or drink by the river.

## MORE BRIDGES

At the end of Boat Quay is **Elgin Bridge** ❺, named after the governor-general of India from 1862 to 1863, Lord James Bruce Elgin. The current concrete structure was completed in 1929, replacing an earlier iron one brought in from India in 1862 and constructed as a link between the Chinese on the south side of the river and the Indian merchants of High Street on the north.

The cruise then passes under the concrete **Coleman Bridge** ❻. Its appearance today is a far cry from the original Palladian-style brick bridge designed by Irish architect George Coleman and built in 1840. The present concrete bridge opened in 1986 to help better cope with heavy traffic flow.

The next bridge is **Read Bridge** ❼, built in 1889 and named after businessman and legislator William Henry Read. In the early days Chinese storytellers entertained Chinese labourers with classic tales of history and chivalry on this bridge.

## RIVERSIDE POINT

If you have bought a river taxi ticket, alight at the Riverside Point jetty. **Clarke Quay Central** ❽ (www.clarkequaycentral.com. sg; daily 11am–10pm) is a short walk away, and is a Japanese-themed mall with boutiques selling streetwear and accessories. Sip a cup of local tea at **Ya Kun Kaya Toast**, see ❶, or have a bite and drink at the restaurants at **Riverside Point** ❾, such as **Café Iguana**, see ❷, or **Brewerkz**, see ❸. Afterwards, cross Read Bridge to Clarke Quay.

## CLARKE QUAY

**Clarke Quay** ❿, spanning five blocks, was named after Lieutenant-General Sir Andrew Clarke, the second governor of the Straits Settlement. Until the 1970s, it hummed with activity as bumboats carried cargo from ships to the warehouses on its banks.

Take a stroll around and discover some of its history. At its southern end, for instance, on the wall of the last shophouse is a sign proclaiming that it was once Whampoa's Ice House. A wealthy Chinese landowner, Whampoa gifted the land where the Singapore Botanic Gardens sits today to the British, who gave him the land at Clarke Quay in return.

Today's Clarke Quay beats to a different tune, with its restored warehouses housing restaurants and notable clubs like Attica (see page 121). The area is pleasant to stroll around in; huge canopies provide cool shade over its lanes in the day and are stunningly lit at night, while lily-pad platforms offer pleasant alfresco dining over the river. If you have

*Robertson Quay*

not had dinner, consider **The Pump Room**, see ❹.

## ROBERTSON QUAY

If you have opted for the 45-minute river cruise, your boat will take you to **Robertson Quay ⓫**. In the old days, this part of the riverbank was filled with warehouses. Now it has been mostly taken over by luxury apartments. The 19th-century warehouses that remain have been restored and are occupied by bars and restaurants.

The boat goes past the **Singapore Tyler Print Institute ⓬** (www. stpi.com.sg; Tue–Fri 10am–7pm, Sat 9am–6pm; free), a gallery with interesting print exhibitions.

### *Alkaff Bridge*

After the print institute, the boat passes under the pedestrian **Alkaff Bridge ⓭**, named after the wealthy Arab Alkaff family. Completed in 1997, the bridge was painted by the late Filipino artist Pacita Abad with help from a team of rope specialists, using 50 different colours and 900 litres of paint.

The boat turns around near the Grand Copthorne Waterfront hotel and then makes its way back to the Merlion Park.

## Food and drink

### ❶ YA KUN KAYA TOAST

Clarke Quay Central 01-31; tel: 6534 7332; www.yakun.com; daily 7am–10pm; $
Have a cup of local tea or coffee at this outlet. If you are feeling peckish, order a crispy stack of kaya toast (toast with coconut jam).

### ❷ CAFÉ IGUANA

01-03 Riverside Point; tel: 6236 1275; www. cafeiguana.com; Mon–Thu 4pm–midnight, Fri until 1am, Sat noon–1am, Sun noon–midnight; $$
This lively restaurant is always packed, thanks to its delicious quesadillas, tortillas and salsas, and cheap margaritas during Happy Hour. It also offers over 150 types of Webber blue agave tequila.

### ❸ BREWERKZ

01-05/06 Riverside Point; tel: 6438 7438; www.brewerkz.com; Sun–Thu noon–midnight, Fri–Sat until 1am; $$$
This microbrewery-restaurant produces over 2,500 hectolitres of handcrafted beer annually. American-style dishes from the Deep South, the Southwest and California are served.

### ❹ THE PUMP ROOM

01-09/10 The Foundry, Clarke Quay; tel: 6334 2628; www.pumproomasia.com.sg; Sun–Fri 6pm–3am, Sat 6pm–4am; $$$
The hearty Australian-inspired fare at this microbrewery and bistro includes crispy blue swimmer crab cake, burgers and a variety of Australian steaks. Try the freshly brewed speciality beers.

# CENTRAL BUSINESS DISTRICT

*The modern and the traditional collide and coalesce in Singapore's financial district. On this route, gaze at gleaming skyscrapers, admire quirky sculptures, view feng shui–friendly architectural features, and visit age-old places of worship.*

> **DISTANCE:** 2.5km (1.5 miles)
> **TIME:** Half a day
> **START:** Raffles Place
> **END:** Telok Ayer Chinese Methodist Church
> **POINTS TO NOTE:** Start your tour after 9.30pm or 2pm to avoid the crowds.

The Central Business District runs close to the Marina Bay waterfront from the Singapore River to Keppel Road. Soaring towers of finance and business line its main arterials of Shenton Way, Robinson Road, Anson Road, Cecil Street and Battery Road. The tallest buildings are centred around **Raffles Place ❶**, a buzzing open-air plaza with the Raffles Place MRT station underground.

In the early days Raffles Place was known as Commercial Square, originally conceived by Stamford Raffles as part of his 1822 town plan. Grand structures housing banks and offices stood here, overlooking a landscaped centre with trees and flower beds.

Also an important shopping destination for upper-crust society, Commercial Square was where Singapore's first department store, Robinsons, was founded in 1858. Destroyed in a fire in 1972, it now has outlets in Orchard Road (see page 64) and Raffles City (see page 32).

## SKYSCRAPERS

A few notable skyscrapers surround Raffles Place, all measuring 280m (920ft) tall (the maximum height allowed by the aviation authorities): OUB Centre, Republic Plaza and UOB Plaza.

Japanese architect Kisho Kurokawa designed the dark, glazed **Republic Plaza ❷**, at the end of D'Almedia Street. This tapering tower won him the World Best Architecture Award from FIABCI in 1997.

From Raffles Place turn left onto Chulia Street. The twin towers of **UOB Plaza ❸**, one of the most recognised icons of the city skyline, were designed by another Japanese architect, Kenzo

*Incense coils at the Wak Hai Cheng Temple*

Tange. He fused his vision with that of Lim Chong Keat, his counterpart for the original octagonal 38-storey UOB Building, adding more levels that are turned at 45 degrees relative to one another, to give the building a unique chiselled look.

Continue along Chulia Street as far as South Canal Road. You will reach **OCBC Centre** ❹, designed by I.M. Pei.

This 52-storey, the first foreigner-designed skyscraper after independence, was completed in 1976. Nicknamed 'the Calculator', it has three distinctive tiers separating windows that resemble button pads. Henry Moore's *Reclining Figure* (see page 54) stands in front of OCBC Centre.

Opposite OCBC Centre is Boat Quay (see page 49). On Circular Road stands **Molly Malone's**, see ❶, good for pub grub.

## WAK HAI CHENG TEMPLE

After lunch, backtrack on South Canal Road and continue on Philip Street. At the corner with Church Street is the **Wak Hai Cheng Temple** ❺ (daily 6am–6pm), built in the 1850s by the Teochew community for the protection of traders travelling between Singapore and China. A constellation of deities, including Ma Chu Po, the Goddess of the Sea, and the Eight Immortals, are enshrined here. Suspended in the forecourt are large coils of incense, which can take up to 10 days to burn.

*Diorama at the Fu Tak Chi Museum*

Cross Church Street to **Capital Square ⑥**, an office block with a feature of cascading water, presumably installed to invite prosperity, for in Chinese belief, water is wealth.

## FAR EAST SQUARE

Take the path between Capital Square and China Street. Ahead is **Ya Kun**, see ②, an institution for *kaya* (coconut jam) toast. Enter **Far East Square ⑦** by the Metal Gate, one of the complex's five gates, each representing an element of the Chinese universe: metal, wood, water, fire and earth.

Far East Square is a conservation area of restored shophouses in four architectural styles prevalent from the 1840s to 1960s – Early, First Transitional, Late and Second Transitional. Bounded by Cross, Telok Ayer and China streets, the complex houses mainly offices and restaurants.

Follow the signs, through a glass door, to the **Fu Tak Chi Museum ⑧** (daily 10am–10pm), formerly a Taoist temple set up by Hakka and Cantonese immigrants in 1824. It displays artefacts donated by early Chinatown residents.

## TELOK AYER STREET

From the museum, turn right on Telok Ayer Street. Meaning 'water bay' in Malay, this street once stood by the shore. Its shophouses are mainly of the First Transitional style, with narrow fronts and modest ornamentation.

### Nagore Durgha Building

At the corner with Boon Tat Street is the **Nagore Durgha Building ⑨**, built in the late 1820s by Tamil Muslims as a meeting place and house of worship. With its intricate minarets, arches and

---

## Public art

A handful of sculptures are peppered around the CBD. Close to the riverside entrance of Raffles Place is Taiwanese sculptor Yang Ying-Feng's monumental *Progress and Advancement*, a celebration of the city's commercial life commissioned by the late banker Lien Ying Chow. Salvador Dali's bronze *Homage to Newton* is found in the ground-floor atrium of UOB Plaza. Just outside the atrium stands the voluptuous bronze Bird, by Columbian artist Fernando Botero, which was inspired by the dove, the universal symbol of peace. Outside OCBC Centre is British sculptor Henry Moore's *Reclining Figure*. When it was first installed, it suffered from corrosion caused by the humid climate, and was subsequently treated to acquire the golden hue it wears today. There are also other bronze sculptures, which depict life in the early days, along the Singapore River.

---

*Telok Ayer shophouses*

niches, it has been described as a multi-layered wedding cake.

### Thian Hock Keng Temple

The next place of worship is the **Thian Hock Keng Temple** ⑩, the Temple of Heavenly Happiness (www.thianhockkeng.com.sg; daily 7.30am–5.30pm). Hokkien immigrants set up a joss house in the 1820s in gratitude to Ma Chu Po for their safe arrival. This became the Thian Hock Keng, built in 1842 without a single nail. Dragons, venerated for protection on sea voyages, adorn the roofs and pillars.

### Al Abrar Mosque

The **Al Abrar Mosque** ⑪ (daily 5–7am and 11.30am–9pm) is a few doors down. Built in the mid-1850s by the Indian Chulia community, it replaced the thatched hut that had been established on the same site in 1827.

Further along is the **Amoy Street Food Centre**, see ③.

### Telok Ayer Methodist Church

Follow the curve of the road. The **Telok Ayer Chinese Methodist Church** ⑫ (www.tacmc.org.sg; Mon–Fri 9am–5pm, Sat until 1pm), on your left, was completed in 1925 and combines Chinese and Western elements – a flat-roofed Chinese pavilion with Art Deco windows and European-style columns. Go through the Telok Ayer Park and turn left on Maxwell Road to reach the underground Tanjong Pagar MRT station, which is on the right after Wallich Street.

## Food and drink

### ① MOLLY MALONE'S

56 Circular Road; tel: 6536 2029; www.molly-malone.com; Mon–Wed 11am–1am, Thu 11am–2am, Fri 11am–3am, Sat noon–2am; $$

At this Irish pub, enjoy excellent pub grub, such as fish and chips, shepherd's pie and Irish lamb stew.

### ② YA KUN KAYA TOAST

01-01 Far East Square; tel: 6438 3638; www.yakun.com; Mon–Fri 7.30am–7pm, Sat 7.30am–4.30pm, Sun 8.30am–3pm; $

Established in 1944, Ya Kun serves a unique Singapore-style breakfast or teatime snack of soft-boiled eggs and kaya toast (grilled bread with coconut jam and butter).

### ③ AMOY STREET FOOD CENTRE

7 Maxwell Road; $

This market and food centre is great for local fare such as minced-meat noodles (noodles tossed with a chilli-vinegar sauce and topped with minced pork) and *char kway teow* (fried rice noodles with cockles).

*Autumn festival lights*

# CHINATOWN

*Like the city's other ethnic enclaves, Chinatown appeals with its fascinating blend of cultures. Visit a mosque, Hindu shrine and Buddhist temple, and explore Chinatown's intriguing narrow streets, traditional shops and market stalls.*

> **DISTANCE:** 1.5km (1 mile)
> **TIME:** Half a day
> **START:** Jamae Mosque
> **END:** Singapore City Gallery
> **POINTS TO NOTE:** Take a taxi to Jamae Mosque at the corner of Mosque Street and South Bridge Road. Alternatively, take the MRT to the Chinatown station. The mosque is a short walk away.

It may seem odd that Singapore, with its majority Chinese population, has a Chinatown. The neighbourhood only came to be known by this name as a result of the tourism board's efforts to promote the city's ethnic enclaves, although it has existed since the early days, when Chinese immigrants congregated south of the Singapore River.

Today's Chinatown is hemmed in by the soaring high-rises of the CBD, but vestiges of the traditional can still be seen. Conservation shophouses hold decades-old businesses, which stand shoulder to shoulder with even older places of worship. Medical halls dispense herbal cures, and exotic smells, from rare Asian ingredients in the fresh-produce market to the pungent aroma of the durian fruit, still dominate the area.

## JAMAE MOSQUE

Chinatown has its share of Chinese temples, but it also has some of the most well-known places of worship of other faiths. This walk starts on South Bridge Road at the **Jamae Mosque** ❶ (daily 9.30am–6pm). Built in 1826 by Tamil Muslims, it sports an eclectic mix of architectural styles, with pagoda-like minarets, a South India-style entrance gate and neoclassical prayer halls.

## SRI MARIAMMAN TEMPLE

Cross Pagoda Street to the **Sri Mariamman Temple** ❷ (daily 7am–noon and 6–9pm). The temple was built in 1827 by Naraina Pillai, who accompanied Raffles on his second visit to Singapore in 1819. Dedicated to the goddess Mariamman, known for curing serious illnesses, it has a *gopuram* (tower)

*Roof details of the Sri Mariamman Temple*

adorned with vivid renditions of Hindu deities at the entrance. If you happen to be here on the holy days of Tuesday and Friday, you can see brightly clad devotees offering *puja* (prayers). This temple is the site of the celebrations for Theemithi, the annual fire-walking festival that takes place around October/November.

Across South Bridge Road from Sri Mariamman Temple is **Eu Yan Sang**, a traditional Chinese medicine business that dates back to 1879. 'Eu' is the name of the family that founded it, and 'Yan Sang' means 'caring for mankind' in Cantonese. The shop stocks over 1,000 types of Chinese herbs and medicinal products, some of which, like herbal candies and bottled bird's-nest soup, make interesting souvenirs.

## CHINATOWN HERITAGE CENTRE

Walk down **Pagoda Street**. Tucked among the many brightly coloured shop-houses, at no. 48, is the **Chinatown Heritage Centre** ❸ (https://chinatownheritagecentre.com.sg; daily 9am–8pm). Using authentic furniture, utensils and other paraphernalia, the museum brings to life the harsh living conditions of Chinatown residents in the early years.

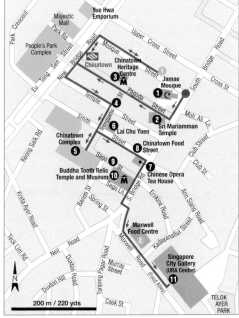

## TRENGGANU AND SMITH STREETS

Turn right on New Bridge Road and then right again onto **Mosque Street**. If you're feeling pecking, head to **Momma Kong's**, see ①, which specialises in crab and crayfish dishes. After your meal, retrace your steps, past Pagoda Street, and turn left onto Temple Street. You then come to the

*Shopping for Chinese New Year decorative ornaments*

junction with **Trengganu Street** ❹, previously an opera street with theatre stages and brothels. Today, you will find over 200 stalls at the Chinatown Street Market (daily 10am–10pm), sprawling over Trengganu, Pagoda, and Sago streets, which are all fully pedestrianised. Here you can pick up trinkets, tourist souvenirs and traditional Chinese goods like calligraphy and masks. In the days leading up to Chinese New Year, this whole area teems with stalls selling all manner of festive goodies, cured meats, mandarin oranges and auspicious decorations.

Turn right onto Trengganu Street. At the corner with Smith Street is **Chinatown Complex** ❺. This is perhaps one of the best places to catch glimpses of local life. At its basement, market vendors sell all manner of fresh produce and dried goods. Upstairs is a food centre with plenty of stalls dishing up excellent, old-fashioned hawker fare.

Diagonally opposite Chinatown Complex on Trengganu Street is **Lai Chun Yuen** ❻, a former Chinese opera house dating back to the 1920s. This is one of the earliest three-storey buildings in the area, with a verandah running around the top level. It is now a budget hotel.

Further along **Smith Street** is the **Chinese Opera Tea House** ❼ (no. 5; tel: 6323 4862; www.ctcopera.com.sg; Tue–Sat noon–5pm, Sun 2–6pm). Here you can have tea and snacks at traditional Chinese tables, surrounded by displays of opera costumes. On Fri-

day and Saturday from 7pm to 9pm, you can enjoy dinner here whilst watching Cantonese opera excerpts (booking advised).

*Chinatown Food Street*
Street hawkers have made a comeback at the open-air **Chinatown Food Street** ❽ (http://chinatown foodstreet.sg; daily 11am–11pm) along Smith Street. Have a bite if hunger pangs strike or return here in the evening to sample local staples like *char kway teow* (fried flat rice noodles) and fish ball noodles. The high-ceiling glass canopy shelter and internal spot cooling system offers comfortable dining whether rain or shine.

## SAGO STREET

Walk down Smith Street and turn right on South Bridge Road. A few steps away is **Sago Street** ❾. Named after the numerous sago factories that operated here in the 1840s, the street was also a red-light district in the early 20th century. Today it is a pedestrian-only lane flanked by shophouses housing old-style Chinese medical halls and pastry shops on one side and souvenir and clothing stalls on the other.

## BUDDHA TOOTH RELIC TEMPLE

Sandwiched between Sago Street and Sago Lane is the **Buddha Tooth Relic Temple and Museum** ❿ (www.

*Buddha Tooth Relic Temple*  *The temple contrasting with the CBD*

btrts.org.sg; daily 7am–7pm; free). Its architecture, interiors and statuary are inspired by the styles of the Tang dynasty – a golden age for Buddhism in China. The temple's centrepiece is one of the Buddha's sacred teeth, an object dogged by much controversy; its authenticity has been doubted by Buddhism scholars and some members of the public. It is held on the fourth floor in a golden stupa and only taken out for viewing on Vesak Day and Chinese New Year. More than half of the 420kg (930lbs) of gold needed to construct the stupa was donated by devotees. It is unveiled for viewing two times a day (9am and 3pm).

Entering the 80m (260ft) -high **100 Dragons Hall** on the ground level, you see an intricately carved 5m (20ft) -tall Maitreya Buddha image. A hundred other Buddha statues line both sides of the hall. On the third floor is the climate-controlled **Buddhist Culture Museum** (daily 9am–6pm), with precious Buddha images collected from all over Asia. On the roof you can admire the *Dendrobium Buddha Tooth*, an orchid hybrid named after the temple, and turn the huge prayer wheel in the **Ten Thousand Buddha Pavilion**.

### SINGAPORE CITY GALLERY

After your temple visit, cross South Bridge Road to the **Maxwell Food Centre**, see ②, for some refreshments before continuing along Maxwell Road to the **Singapore City Gallery** ⓫ (www. ura.gov.sg/gallery; Mon–Sat 9am–5pm; free) at the URA Centre.

The gallery's highlight is an enormous scaled and detailed 11x11m (36x36ft) architectural model of Singapore's central area. The rest of the gallery's 50 exhibits are spread over two storeys, including a multimedia exhibit that charts Singapore's architectural development over the past 180 years. You can also survey the vision the planners have for the island in the 21st century.

## Food and drink

### ① MOMMA KONG'S

34 Mosque Street; tel: 6225 2722; www. mommakongs.com; Mon–Fri 5–11pm, Sat–Sun 11am–11pm; $$$

Located in a narrow shophouse, Momma Kong's specialises in crab, deshelled or otherwise, and crayfish prepared in a variety of styles, such as red chilli or butter.

### ② MAXWELL FOOD CENTRE

Corner of South Bridge Road and Maxwell Road; daily 7am–10pm; $

This bustling food centre is a great place for dining round the clock from breakfast through to supper. Stalls that often have a queue are Zhen Zhen (no. 54) for its congee and Tian Tian (no. 10) for its chicken rice.

# ORCHARD ROAD

*No visit to Singapore is complete without a day's retail therapy on its most famous shopping artery, dense with ritzy malls and sidewalk cafés. The strip also has an enclave with exquisite Chinese Baroque-style houses.*

**DISTANCE:** 3km (2 miles), not including the distances covered in the malls
**TIME:** A full day
**START:** Tanglin Mall
**END:** MacDonald House
**POINTS TO NOTE:** To get to Tanglin Mall, at the corner of Tanglin and Grange roads, take a taxi or bus no. 36, which stops in front of The Regent hotel. Most shops and malls open at 10.30 or 11am and close at 9 or 10pm.

The famous Orchard Road was so named because of the many nutmeg, pepper and fruit plantations found here in the 1800s. In the 1840s the area was also dotted with cemeteries. But by the 20th century, Orchard metamorphosed into a vibrant commercial centre and later into the city's most upmarket address, teeming with malls and luxury hotels. The city's passion for shopping is easily demonstrated by the numerous, overcrowded malls on Orchard Road. It would be too exhausting to visit all the shopping centres in a day; this tour takes you through

the shopping highlights and a few historical sights, starting from the Tanglin area.

## TANGLIN ROAD

Begin with a fortifying brunch at **Caffe Beviamo**, see ❶, in **Tanglin Mall ❶**, which has boutiques and gourmet-food shops.

From Tanglin Mall, walk up Tanglin Road as far as **Tudor Court ❷**. If you are interested in Asian artefacts and antiques, a few of the shops here are worth a browse. The upscale French gourmet store Hédiard is also here, with caviar, wines, preserves, teas and spices. Continue past **St Regis Hotel** and on to **Tanglin Shopping Centre ❸**. The latter's dated exterior belies the quality antiques and art found in its galleries and shops.

## FORUM, HILTON AND FOUR SEASONS

Follow the bend around Orchard Parade Hotel into Orchard Road proper. On the right is **Forum The**

*Orchard Road, packed with shoppers*

**Shopping Mall** ④, filled with boutiques for children and mothers.

Further on from Forum, look out for the two Chinese warrior statues in front of the **Hilton Hotel** ⑤. These 'doorway guardians' are said to offer protection from evil spirits. The Shopping Gallery Hilton Singapore is a good stop for designer jewellery and haute couture in the likes of Issey Miyake and Lanvin.

It also connects to the **Four Seasons Hotel's shopping arcade** just behind. The **Club 21** gallery here features Balenciaga, Mulberry, Marc Jacobs and other luxe fashion labels.

*Palais Renaissance and around*
Opposite the Hilton is the swanky **Palais Renaissance** ⑥, with a number of select boutiques and Passion Hair Salon frequented by local celebrities and well-heeled ladies.

When King Chulalongkorn visited Singapore in the 1890s, he bought the property next to the Palais Renaissance. Today, this is the Thai Embassy (www.thaiembassy.sg). It hosts an annual Thai Festival in its spacious garden in June, during which you can catch a whiff of pungent durians even from a distance.

On the opposite side, after the ageing Far East Shopping Centre, is **Liat Towers** ⑦, which hosts the Spanish brands Zara and Massimo Dutti as well as luxury label Hermès. Beside it is **Wheelock Place** ⑧, designed by Japanese superstar architect Kisho Kurokawa. Its glass pyramid is a landmark. A variety of speciality shops and eateries can be found here.

### SCOTTS ROAD

Cross the road to **Shaw Centre** ⑨, home to the Japanese department store Isetan, as well as Lido Cineplex, which underwent a major refurbishment and now houses 11 cinemas including Singapore's first and only IMAX's Digital Theatre System.

Further on Scotts Road, past Royal Plaza on Scotts hotel, is the striking red **T Galleria by DFS** ⑩, which stocks a wide variety of duty-free goods, from high-end clothing to kitschy souvenirs.

## The Istana

The Istana (www.istana.gov.sg), meaning 'palace' in Malay, is the seat and official residence of Singapore's president, Halimah Yacob. Built in 1869, the elegant neo-Palladian Anglo-Indian building was once the British governor's residence. During the Japanese occupation, it was used by Japanese army commanders. The grounds of the Istana are open to the public from 8.30am to 6pm on Labour Day, Hari Raya Puasa, National Day, Deepavali and Chinese New Year. Foreigners need to pay a $2 entrance fee. On the first Sunday of every month, a changing-of-guards ceremony takes place at the main gate from 5.45pm.

*Goodwood Park*

### Far East Plaza

Take the overhead bridge to the **Far East Plaza** ⓫. Its eclectic hole-in-the-wall shops target teens looking for affordable streetwear but there is also no lack of bespoke tailors, tattoo parlours and karaoke pubs. Though the building has not worn its years well, it is still a great place for bargains.

### Goodwood Park Hotel

Far East Plaza is sandwiched between **Goodwood Park Hotel** ⓬ and the Grand Hyatt. Designed by Swan and MacLaren after the castles along the River Rhine, the Goodwood Park was originally built as the Teutonia Club in 1900 for the German community.

During World War I, the club was seized as enemy property and then auctioned off to three Jewish brothers who turned it into a performance venue, christening it Goodwood Hall. One of its highlights came in 1922 with a performance by one of the world's greatest ballerinas, Anna Pavlova.

In 1929 the hall was converted into a hotel. The Japanese used it as their military headquarters during their occupation, and in 1945 the British turned it into a war-crimes court. Its Grand Tower, which became a national monument in 1989, has notable architectural elements such as fluted columns, delicate woodwork and graceful archways.

On the other side of Far East Plaza is the **Grand Hyatt** ⓭, which has angled

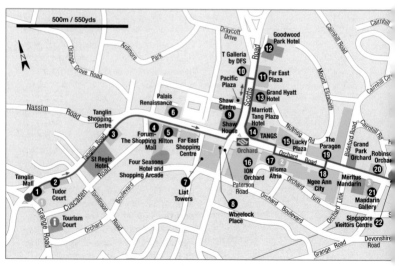

*Singapore Visitor's Centre*

*The futuristic ION Orchard mall*

doors and a Zen-inspired fountain in its lobby. These features were reportedly designed to address *feng shui* concerns; the hotel is said to have flourished after they were installed.

## THE MAIN STRETCH

At the junction of Scotts and Orchard roads is the pagoda-like **Marriott Tang Plaza Hotel** ⑭. Adjoining it is **TANGS** department store, noted for its cult skincare brands and kitchen gadgets. TANGS was founded by C.K. Tang, who arrived in Singapore from China in 1922. Among the first to recognise the potential of Orchard Road, Tang was unperturbed by the presence of a Chinese

cemetery opposite the store's location. In fact, business flourished and outgrew the original smaller building. Next door is **Lucky Plaza** ⑮. It is tatty around the edges but still popular for its bargain-basement electronic goods.

Situated opposite TANGS is **ION Orchard** ⑯. This swanky mall houses the flagship stores of numerous luxury brands such as Prada, Miu Miu and Marc Jacobs, as well as many food outlets. Head up to ION SKY on the 56th floor for 360-degree views of Singapore through special telescopes.

Next to ION is the Orchard MRT station. Further on is the fashion-centred **Wisma Atria** ⑰, with a branch of the Japanese department store Isetan and numerous high-street fashion boutiques. A good lunch spot here is **Food Republic**, see ②.

Linked by an underpass to Wisma Atria is the oversized **Ngee Ann City** ⑱ with boutiques selling everything from haute couture to street fashion. Its anchor tenant, **Takashimaya** department store, has a wonderful food hall, purveying delicacies from the world over. **Books Kinokuniya** on the fourth floor stocks all manner of books and magazines. On the same floor, there are a few art galleries and stylish stationers.

Unbridled consumerism continues across the road in **The Paragon** ⑲, filled with boutiques of top international designer names such as Gucci, Prada, Salvatore Ferragamo and Tod's. Also located here are Marks & Spencer, Toys 'R' Us and a good range of eateries.

*Signage at Centrepoint*

Opposite The Paragon is Grand Park Orchard Hotels's Knightsbridge, housing retail stores such as Abercrombie & Fitch and Tommy Hilfiger. Further along is **Robinsons Orchard** ⑳, which has taken over the entire Heeren building and filled it with all manner of mid to high-end fashion, beauty, home and lifestyle brands.

Opposite the Heeren is the Meritus Mandarin Hotel and its stylish shopping arcade, **Mandarin Gallery** ㉑. There are various well-known boutiques here. Food-wise, there are several good outlets such as the famous **Ippudo SG** ramen eateries from Japan, see ❸.

### Tourist information
Swing by the **Singapore Visitors Centre** ㉒ (daily 8.30am–9.30pm), at the junction of Cairnhill and Orchard roads, where you can get information on sights, book tours and buy event tickets.

### EMERALD HILL

The Somerset MRT station is close by, if you want to call it a day. Opposite the station is **Peranakan Place** ㉓, a complex of highly ornamented Straits Chinese terrace houses. You can relax at its shaded terrace café with a refreshing drink. Then explore the lovely Chinese Baroque-style terrace houses further up the slope, on **Emerald Hill** ㉔.

The 30 double-storey terrace houses on Emerald Hill, built between 1901 and 1925, have thankfully not been razed but carefully restored, having been accorded conservation status in the 1980s, which means their owners are not allowed to alter their facades.

Look out for ceramic tiles with intricate flower motifs, ornamental mouldings, and carved swing doors with gold patterns. Check out no. 83 for its original facade with pastel blue wood and white tiles, and no. 73, which has intricate gold paintwork on its wooden shutters.

The value of these houses is sky-high, and many are rented out to well-heeled expatriates. You may be able to peek inside some of these plush homes if the doors are ajar. The majority of these upscale residences have a courtyard; a few of them even have small indoor swimming pools.

There are also a few watering holes on Emerald Hill. Establishments such as **No. 5** (tel: 6732 0818), **Ice Cold Beer** (see page 123) and the atmospheric **Alley Bar** (see page 122) are longstanding favourites. **Que Pasa**, see ❹, is great for tapas and sangria.

### CENTREPOINT

If you still have the time and energy for more shopping, step into one of the older but still popular malls, **Centrepoint** ㉕, where the Metro department store boasts six levels of fashion and lifestyle products.

### Orchard Central
Opposite Centrepoint is **Orchard Central** ㉖, a retail development dedicated

*House on Emerald Hill*                    *A wealth of brands*

to Asian brands. The mall itself can be a little hard to navigate. The Orchard Central site has an interesting history. In the 1970s it was Glutton's Square, a popular open-air street-dining spot. The food stalls were revived during the 2004 Singapore Food Festival but have since been relocated next to The Esplanade and renamed Makansutra Gluttons Bay.

Adjacent to Orchard Central is **orchardgateway** ㉗, the only mall that straddles both sides of Orchard Road. High-street fashion brands, indie fashion stores and blogshops are found here. The two buildings which also house a hotel and offices are connected via a glass tubular bridge and underpass. Next door is **313 Somerset** ㉘, which has a massive Food Republic Food Court. Somerset MRT is just below this mall.

## DHOBY GHAUT

A 10-minute walk from Centrepoint brings you to the **Istana** ㉙, the Singapore president's official residence. Opposite is the leafy **Istana Park** ㉚, with its pretty landscaping. Its centrepiece is the Festival Arch, a structure with banners, flags and a design that echoes the Istana entrance.

Beside the Istana is yet another mall, **Plaza Singapura** ㉛, with Golden Village cinemas and Japan's two-dollar store, Daiso. Next door is **The Atrium@ Orchard** ㉜, linked to the Dhoby Ghaut MRT station by an underpass.

**MacDonald House** ㉝, one of the oldest multistorey office buildings in this area, stands next to The Atrium, and the adjoining buildings mark the end of Orchard Road.

## Food and drink

**① CAFFE BEVIAMO**

163 Tanglin Road; tel: 6738 7906; https://caffebeviamo.com; daily 9am–9pm; $$
Generously portioned sandwiches, salads, antipasti and pastas.

**② FOOD REPUBLIC**

Wisma Atria, 435 Orchard Road; tel: 6737 9881; https://foodrepublic.com.sg; daily 10am–10pm; $
This massive food court underwent a major revamp in 2017, but its decoration still evokes the Singapore of yesteryear.

**③ IPPUDO SG**

Mandarin Gallery, 333A Orchard Road; tel: 6235 2797; www.ippudo.com.sg; Mon–Sat 11am–11pm, Sun 11am–10pm; $$
This famous ramen eatery from Japan sees long queues at meal times, so get there early.

**④ QUE PASA**

7 Emerald Hill Road; tel: 6235 6626; www.quepasa.com.sg; Mon–Thu 1.30pm–2am, Fri–Sat until 3am, Sun 5.30pm–2am; $$
This Spanish-inspired bar serves sangria and a good range of wines as well as delicious tapas.

*Orchid blooms*

# BOTANIC GARDENS AND TANGLIN VILLAGE

*The Botanic Gardens, a lush green lung minutes away from Orchard Road, offers luxuriant trees, virgin jungle and a fabulous orchid garden. Close by, you'll find Tanglin Village, with its stylish restaurants and antiques shops.*

**DISTANCE:** 3.5km (2 miles)
**TIME:** 3–4 hours
**START:** Botanic Gardens
**END:** Tanglin Village
**POINTS TO NOTE:** Do this walk in the early morning or late afternoon when the air is fresher and the weather cooler. The main Tanglin Gate entrance to the Botanic Gardens is at the junction of Holland and Napier roads. This walk starts at the Central Core, accessed via the Nassim Gate entrance on Cluny Road. The nearest MRT station is Orchard. From there, take a taxi to the Visitor Centre at the junction of Nassim and Cluny roads.

The first botanic garden in Singapore was established in 1822 on Fort Canning Hill by Stamford Raffles as an experimental station for commercial cultivation. Its most notable crop was the Pará rubber tree (*Hevea brasiliensis*), from Brazil, introduced by Henry Ridley, who went on to establish Malaya's rubber industry.

## BOTANIC GARDENS

The present 64-hectare (158-acre) **Singapore Botanic Gardens** (www.sbg.org.sg; daily 5am–midnight; free) was founded by an agri-horticultural society in 1859 and subsequently handed over to the colonial administration for maintenance. Today the gardens contain over 3,000 species of trees and shrubs, in areas as varied as virgin jungle, marshland, lakes and formal gardens. It is also a centre for horticultural and botanical research and experimentation, with an emphasis on orchid breeding and hybridisation.

Before you begin your walk, grab a bite at **Casa Verde**, see ❶, located at the **Visitor Centre ❶**. After your meal, go through the Palm Court, with cascading water features and palm trees; veer right and walk towards the Evolution Garden.

### Evolution Garden

The **Evolution Garden ❷** (daily 5am–7pm) is a cleverly designed garden, with landscaping that chronicles the evolution of plants from the pre-historic times

till the present day. Rock formations are interspersed among ferns and trees that are rarely found on the streets of modern cities. Look out for the curious-looking giant clubmosses (*epidodendrons*), the prehistoric equivalent of trees today, and the stone columns of 'petrified' tree trunks, which are the fossilised remains of ancient trees.

Leave the Evolution Garden and retrace your steps to the Palm Court and past a restored 1920s black-and-white colonial bungalow, which houses the fine-dining restaurant **Corner House**.

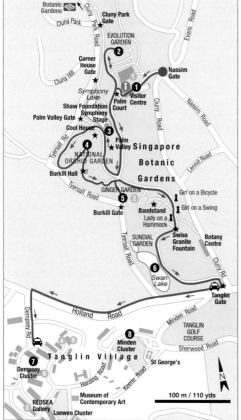

Continue on Heliconia Walk. From here you can see the **Shaw Foundation Symphony Stage ❸**, flanked by the **Symphony Lake** and the rolling lawns of the **Palm Valley**, which teem with picnickers during the occasional weekend concerts.

### National Orchid Garden

Head down Upper Palm Valley Road to the **National Orchid Garden ❹** (daily 8.30am–7pm), whose landscaped grounds are filled with a profusion of gorgeous orchids. It has the largest orchid display in the world with some 1,000 species and 2,000 hybrids, and more are added every year. The meander-

*Water features complement the lush greenery*

ing paths and fountains make this a charming walk.

Highlights include the **VIP Orchid Garden**, with hybrids named after state dignitaries and VIPs, such as Paravanda Nelson Mandela and Vanda William Catherine. Look out for the *Vanda Miss Joaquim*. This hybrid was discovered by Agnes Joaquim in her garden in 1893 and was selected as Singapore's national flower in 1981 because of its hardiness and resilience. Next to the VIP Orchid Garden is **Burkill Hall**, a colonial plantation bungalow built in 1886. It is now used to showcase information on the different hybrids named after the VIPs who have visited the garden. Don't miss the **Cool House**, a simulated tropical montane forest habitat, draped with orchids, epiphytes and carnivorous pitcher plants.

### Ginger Garden

Continue to the **Ginger Garden ⑤** to see a collection of flora from the ginger family, including bananas and heliconias. Head to **Halia**, see ②, for its splendid food.

### Lower Ring Road

Take the Lower Ring Road, along which you will come across a white cast-iron **bandstand**, built in 1930.

Further down Lower Ring Road are a series of **bronze sculptures** by Sydney Harpley: *Girl on a Swing, Girl on a Bicycle* and *Lady on a Hammock*. Completed 1984–1989 and symbolising freedom and exuberance, they were gifted by David Marshall, Singapore's first chief minister, and are dedicated to the children of Singapore.

### Swan Lake

Turn right when you come to the **Swiss Granite Fountain** and walk past the **Sundial Garden** to **Swan Lake ⑥**, with a huge swan sculpture in its heart. Visitors, especially families with children, come here to feed the swans and terrapins.

The path then leads to Tanglin Gate, from where you can exit the gardens.

### TANGLIN VILLAGE

After your Botanic Gardens tour, hop in a taxi to **Tanglin Village** (Dempsey Hill; www.dempsey-hill.com), located off Holland Road (only about five minutes away), for lunch or dinner.

Originally a nutmeg plantation, the area was converted to the Tanglin Barracks, occupied by British troops in the 1860s and later abandoned. In recent years, the barracks have been given a new lease of life and are now a thriving lifestyle and dining destination, organised into three clusters: Dempsey, Minden and Loewen.

### Dempsey Cluster

The **Dempsey Cluster ⑦** is the most developed, with plenty of good restaurants and stores selling Asian-style furniture, artefacts and antiques amid lush greenery. A favourite among locals is the durian stall located in the car park. You can catch scents of the pungent fruit a distance away.

On the other side of the development, both the **REDSEA Gallery** (www.

*Strolling in the serene gardens*

redseagallery.com; daily 11am–8pm) and the **Museum of Contemporary Arts** (www.mocaloewen.sg; daily 11am–7pm) exhibit modern, mostly abstract, works of art.

The Dempsey Cluster offers a carefully curated selection of restaurants. Recommended are **Jones the Grocer**, see ❸; **Samy's Curry**, see ❹; **Long Beach Seafood**, see ❺; and **Roadhouse**, see ❻.

### Minden Cluster

The **Minden Cluster** ❽ is home to the Tanglin Golf Course and the Anglican **St George's Church** (www.stgeorges.org.sg), built in 1911 as a garrison church for British troops. During World War II, the Japanese army used it as an ammunition store. This pretty red-brick building was made a national monument in 1978.

## Food and drink

### ❶ CASA VERDE
Visitors Centre Singapore Botanic Gardens; tel: 6467 7326; www.casaverde.com.sg; Mon–Fri 7.30am–8pm, Sat–Sun 7.30am–9pm; $$
This alfresco spot serves both local and Italian cuisine. Breakfast and an all-day dining menu including wood-fired pizzas are also available.

### ❷ HALIA
Ginger Garden, Botanic Gardens; tel: 8444 1148; www.thehalia.com; Mon–Thu 9am–9.30pm, Fri 9am–10pm, Sat 10am–10pm, Sun 10am–9.30pm; $$–$$$
Halia ('ginger' in Malay) is nestled amid lush tropical foliage. The all-day menu features modern European fare with Asian flavours.

### ❸ JONES THE GROCER
01-12, Blk 9D Dempsey Road; tel: 6476 1518; www.jonesthegrocer.com; daily 8am–11pm; $$
This Australian gourmet store with a café is a great place for a coffee and a sweet treat.

### ❹ SAMY'S CURRY
25 Dempsey Road; tel: 6472 2080; Wed–Mon 11am–3pm and 6–10pm, $$
Delicious South Indian fare is served on banana leaves. Samy's has a faithful following for its fish-head curry.

### ❺ LONG BEACH SEAFOOD
01-01, 25 Dempsey Road; tel: 6323 2222; www.longbeachseafood.com.sg; daily 11am–3pm and 5pm–1am; $$$
Excellent Singapore-style seafood dishes, including black pepper crab, chilli crab and fried baby squid.

### ❻ ROADHOUSE
13 Dempsey Road; tel: 6476 2922; www.theprivegroup.com.sg/roadhouse; Fri 6–10pm, Sat–Sun 10am–10pm; $$
This modern American 'diner' rolls out substantial burgers, grilled steaks, spare ribs and one-of-a-kind desserts (think: warm salted triple nut pie).

*Shophouses on Arab Street*

# KAMPONG GLAM

*The Arab Quarter has shed its sleepy image with the entry of stylish boutiques and cafés, but its Malay and Middle Eastern essence can still be felt in the dignified mosques and traditional businesses.*

**DISTANCE:** 1.5km (1 mile)
**TIME:** 3–4 hours
**START:** Arab Street
**END:** Bali Lane
**POINTS TO NOTE:** This is recommended as a late-morning-to-afternoon walk as many of the shops only open for business in the afternoon. Take a taxi to Arab Street or the MRT to the Bugis station and walk for 15 minutes to the starting point.

Stamford Raffles allocated this area to Sultan Hussein, the Malay king who ceded the island to the British in 1824. The sultan built a palace here for his family and homes for his retainers. Subsequently Javanese and Minangkabau traders, Arab textile merchants and even Chinese tombstone makers settled here, alongside the Malay community.

The enclave's name means 'village of the *gelam* tree'. The tree's bark was prized for its medicinal value and used by the early Bugis and Malay residents to caulk boats, although it would be difficult to find this tree growing in Singapore today.

This neighbourhood used to run along the shore, with many of its houses built on stilts above the tidal mudflats. Much of Kampong Glam was a mangrove swamp and was drained in the 1820s. Beach Road, as its name suggests, was once a coastal road. In the 1880s reclamation pushed the road further inland.

Today's Kampong Glam extends over the area bordered by Ophir Road, Victoria Street, Jalan Sultan and Beach Road. Its main landmarks are the centuries-old mosques, but lately, it has also drawn a new following with local designer boutiques, cafés and restaurants.

## ARAB STREET

Start your stroll on **Arab Street ❶**. The local shops and eateries are set in restored two-storey shophouses, many of which were built in the Early Shophouse style in the 1840s, resembling

*Rishi Handicrafts' caneware*

unadorned dollhouses with their squat upper levels and simple lines.

Along Arab Street are shops selling ethnic jewellery, alcohol-free perfumes and all manner of fabrics. At the corner of Arab and Baghdad streets is **Rishi Handicrafts** (no. 58), its shopfront displaying baskets and other caneware of every shape, size and colour. Opposite Rishi is **Goodwill Trading** (no. 56), its walls covered with batiks. There are also several shops along this street selling Oriental carpets.

## BUSSORAH STREET

Turn left on Beach Road and pass the fishing tackle shops. Turn left again, onto the narrow **Bussorah Street ②**, lined with eateries and souvenir shops. The British named Bussorah Street after an Iraqi town in order to commemo-

rate their victory against the Turks in World War I. During the Ramadan fasting month before the Muslim celebration of Hari Raya Puasa each year this street bustles with food vendors and their Muslim customers, who buy home-cooked delicacies for breaking their fast at sunset. On the left is **Beirut Grill**, see ①, serving Middle Eastern cuisine.

Further along at no. 21 is a Malay food stall that has been in business without a name on its signage for more than three decades. Many locals come for its *teh tarik* ('pulled' tea), *teh halia* (ginger tea), *nasi lemak* (rice cooked in coconut milk), *pisang goreng* (banana fritters) and Malay cakes.

Past the Bussorah Street junction is **Bussorah Mall**, a quiet pedestrianised street flanked by restored 19th-century shophouses. The Sultan Mosque looms at the end of the street.

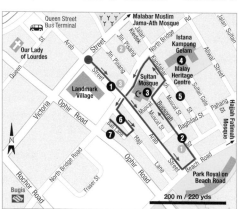

## SULTAN MOSQUE

**Sultan Mosque ③** (www.sultanmosque.sg; Sat–Thu 10am–noon and 2–4pm, Fri 2.30–4pm), distinguished by its golden onion dome and soaring minarets, is the most important place of Muslim worship in Singapore. The first mosque on this site was built in 1824 by Sultan Hussein. The

*Relaxing at a café*

current structure, the largest mosque in Singapore with a 5,000-capacity prayer hall, was completed in 1928. The colonial architect firm Swan and Maclaren adopted the design of the Taj Mahal in India and combined it with Persian, Moorish, Turkish and classical themes.

## Historical mosques

Apart from the grand Sultan Mosque, there are two other mosques in the Arab Quarter that are worth making a detour for. At the corner of Jalan Sultan and Victoria Street you'll see the golden domes of the blue mosaic-tiled **Malabar Muslim Jama-Ath Mosque** (daily 10am–noon and 2–4pm). The mosque, established by Indian Muslims from the Malabar coast of Kerala, harks back to the time when Kampong Glam was founded. Historical records dating from 1836 show that Malay princes were buried in the old Malay cemetery here. Behind Jalan Sultan and off Beach Road is **Hajjah Fatimah Mosque** (daily 9am–9pm), named after a devout Muslim shipping entrepreneur who donated her home to be the site of this mosque. Designed by a British architect, this European-style building, completed in 1846, features a tall minaret and a stained-glass dome. Because its spire tilts at six degrees, the mosque is dubbed Singapore's 'Leaning Tower'.

## MALAY HERITAGE CENTRE

Leave the mosque and turn left onto Kandahar Street, where you will find the **Istana Kampong Gelam**, set in a beautiful garden (Tue–Sun 10am–6pm). Its architecture combines traditional Malay motifs with the Palladian style that dates back to the 1840s.

The **Malay Heritage Centre** ❹ (www.malayheritage.org.sg; Tue–Sun 10am–6pm) is housed in the Istana building and has six permanent galleries showcasing interesting regalia of Malay royalty and artefacts pertaining to Malay history and culture. The adjacent two-storey **Gedung Kuning** ('Yellow Mansion'), originally built for Tengku Mahmoud, grandson of Sultan Hussein, was bought over in 1912 by Haji Yusoff, a Malay entrepreneur and philanthropist in Singapore. His family owned Gedung Kuning until 1999 when the Singapore government acquired the building.

## KANDAHAR STREET

Walk down **Kandahar Street** ❺ towards North Bridge Road. Kandahar Street is named after the city of Kandahar in Afghanistan, originally part of the British empire. The old shophouses here have been accorded conservation status. Their architecture is a fusion of European, Malay, Chinese and Indian elements. Look out for the

*Textiles for sale*

units with swinging doors known as *pintu pagar*.

If you have not had lunch, cross North Bridge Road and turn left towards **Jalan Pisang**. At no. 11 on this street is the **Hajjah Maimunah Restaurant**, see ❷. Further along on North Bridge Road is **Zam Zam** ❸, an institution that serves Muslim Indian food.

## HAJI LANE

Continue on North Bridge Road, go past Arab Street and turn onto **Haji Lane** ❻. Here you will find some seriously hip boutiques that have been opened by young local designers, as well as vintage stores dripping with bohemian charm. One of the best is

**Salad** (no. 25/27 Mon–Sat noon–6pm), proffering home and fashion accessories as well as clothes in mainly black and white colours.

## BALI LANE

Take the small lane that leads from Haji Lane to **Bali Lane** ❼. A nice end to your afternoon is **Blu Jaz Café** (no. 11; www.blujazcafe.net; Mon–Tue 9am–12.30am, Wed–Thu until 1am, Fri–Sat until 2.30am, Sun noon–midnight), a casual restaurant-bar. Linger or return in the evening to catch its live jazz performances.

To leave this area, cross Ophir Road, parallel to Bali Lane; the Bugis MRT station is just ahead.

## Food and drink

### ❶ BEIRUT GRILL
72 Bussorah Street; tel: 6341 7728; http://beirut.com.sg; daily noon–11pm; $$
This Lebanese restaurant serves up Middle Eastern classics like falafel, kebabs and baba ghanoush along with smaller plates such as *warak eneb* vine leaves stuffed with cinnamon rice.

### ❷ HAJJAH MAIMUNAH RESTAURANT
11 &15 Jalan Pisang; tel: 6297 4294; www.hjmaimunah.com; Mon–Sat 7am–8pm; $
This small, modest eatery has a fierce following

so it is usually full. Join the queue and make your choices at the counter. The spread includes tender beef *rendang* (dry curry) stewed in coconut milk, grilled chicken and colourful Malay cakes.

### ❸ SINGAPORE ZAM ZAM RESTAURANT
697–699 North Bridge Road; tel: 6298 6320; http://zamzamsingapore.com; daily 7am–11pm; $
A popular spot serving Indian-Muslim specialties. Tuck into robustly spicy mutton or chicken biryani with aromatic basmati rice, as well as *murtabak* breads, stuffed with minced mutton or chicken.

# LITTLE INDIA

*Take a walk through the most characterful ethnic enclave in Singapore and experience the heart of Singapore's Indian culture with all your senses; discover spirited daily life, heady aromas of spices and enchanting traditional rituals.*

---

**DISTANCE:** 1.5km (1 mile)
**TIME:** 2–3 hours
**START:** Little India Arcade
**END:** Leong San See Temple
**POINTS TO NOTE:** Late morning is a good time to start this route. Take a taxi or the MRT to Little India station, a short walk to the starting point.

---

Little India spreads over the area bounded by Sungei Road, Jalan Besar, Lavender Street and Race Course Road. Running through its heart is **Serangoon Road**, a thoroughfare from which numerous backlanes, lined with small shops spilling over with saris, fabrics and floral garlands, fan out.

The enclave was designated by Stamford Raffles as the Indian district in his 1822 town plan, first thriving as a cattle-rearing ground. It later grew as a hub of Indian commerce, just as it flourishes today, although many of the traditional businesses have made way for contemporary ones. Little India is a magnet for both migrant workers and tourists from the Indian subcontinent.

### BACKSTREETS

Begin your tour at the Art Deco-style **Little India Arcade ❶** and spend some time perusing the stalls selling crafts, jewellery and souvenirs. Exiting the mall, turn left on **Clive Street**, where little shops are crammed with cookware.

Turn left onto **Campbell Lane ❷**. In the arts and craft shops here, you can find a jumble of rugs, soft furnishings, trinkets, Christian icons and Buddha and Ganesh images. At **Jothi Store & Flower Shop** (no. 1; daily 10am–9pm), fragrant jasmine flowers are strung into garlands, to be offered in Hindu temples.

Turn right onto Serangoon Road, which is dotted with restaurants, some of them established since the time when the area was largely populated by single men, whose domestic arrangements did not include private kitchens. Stop by **Ananda Bhavan**, see ❶, for ginger tea and South Indian snacks.

*Sri Veeramakaliamman Temple*

From Serangoon Road, turn right onto **Dunlop Street ❸**. You can see a typical provision shop with interesting Asian fruits and vegetables, from bitter gourd to betel leaves, heaped into crates and baskets that spill over onto the walkway. Spices such as bright yellow turmeric, deep red saffron and mellow brown cinnamon, assail your senses with their aromas and colours.

Tucked away at 41 Dunlop Street is **Abdul Gafoor Mosque** (daily 7am–noon and 2.30–4.30pm), an Arabian- and Renaissance-style mosque, built in 1859. Its prayer hall is decorated with Moorish arches and has a tableau tracing the origins of Islam.

When you have seen enough of Dunlop Street, backtrack to Serangoon Road. This stretch of the thoroughfare contains shops selling multicoloured saris and accessories on both sides. Another Little India institution here is **Komala Vilas**, see ❷, offering good vegetarian food.

## SRI VEERAMAKALIAMMAN TEMPLE

Across the street, past Belilios Road, stands the **Sri Veeramakaliamman Temple ❹** (www.sriveeramakaliamman.com; daily 5.30am–12.30pm and 4–9pm), dating from 1835. It is dedicated to the multi-armed goddess Kali, the manifestation of anger against evil. As consort to Shiva, Kali is also known as Parvati in her benign form. Therefore she is both feared as well as loved. In the main shrine, her statue is flanked by those of her sons – Murugan, the child god, and Ganesh, the Elephant God.

*In Mustafa Centre*

The temple is packed with devotees on the Hindu holy days of Tuesday and Friday. They often break a coconut before entering the temple to denote the breaking of their ego. Cracked shells are tossed into the aluminium receptacles under the *gopuram* (tower). Fresh coconut and mango leaves above the entrance symbolise purity and welcome; the lotus represents a human striving for spiritual perfection; and banana offerings indicate abundance.

## ANGULLIA MOSQUE

Continue along Serangoon Road as far as Birch Road, with another historical place of worship, the **Angullia Mosque** ❺ (daily 4.30–8am and noon–10pm), built over 100 years ago. Cross over to the other side to Syed Alwi Road and visit the decidedly secular phenomenon that is **Mustafa Centre** ❻ (145 Syed Alwi Road; tel: 6295 5855; www.mustafa.com.sg; daily 24 hours), a department store like no other in Singapore. Open around the clock, it stocks the widest selection of merchandise, from the latest power tools to the most obscure toiletries, all heaped bazaar-style. The Mustafa Centre's success has spawned a hotel, café and travel agency, plus an extension of the mall on Verdun Road. The best time to shop here is the wee hours of the morning when the aisles are nearly empty, and the worst is Sunday, when it is really crowded.

Turn right onto **Kampong Kapur Road**, where the garish Royal India Hotel stands, and right again onto **Desker Road**. This street has plenty of cheap hotels and a seedy reputation. Turn right onto **Lembu Road**, where Indian migrant workers in the construction industry congregate on the Lembu Road Open Space.

## SRI SRINIVASA PERUMAL TEMPLE

Turn left onto Syed Alwi Road and make your way to Serangoon Road. It is a good 10-minute walk to the next place of interest. After passing Fortuna Hotel and the Kitchener Road junction, cross to the opposite side. After Perumal Road is the brightly coloured **Sri Srinivasa Perumal Temple** ❼ (daily 6.30am–noon and 6–9pm). It was founded by migrant Naradimhaloo Naidu, who endowed a portion of his property to the temple in 1860. A century later, local philanthropist P. Govindasamy Pillay met the expenses for the adding of the five-tier *gopuram* (tower), which rises 21m (70ft) above the entrance. Figures on the *gopuram* depict the various incarnations of Vishnu, also known as Perumal, the Preserver of Life, who appears on Earth in different forms.

### Thaipusam

Each year during Thaipusam, around January or February, a procession of devotees begins at the Sri Srinivasa Perumal Temple and ends at the Chettiar Temple on Tank Road. The men pierce their tongues, cheeks and bodies with skewers that support their *kavadi*, heavy arched steel

*Jewellery boxes*

structures decorated with peacock feathers. Women devotees participating in the procession carry jugs of milk on their heads. These acts of faith are performed either as penance or in gratitude to Lord Murugan, Shiva's son.

Leave the temple and follow the adjacent path, past blocks of public housing and a tiny playground, to **Race Course Road**.

### SAKYA MUNI BUDDHA GAYA TEMPLE

Little India may be the hub of the Hindu community, but, reflective of Singapore's multicultural outlook, it also has places of worship of various faiths.

To your right is the **Sakya Muni Buddha Gaya Temple** ❽ (daily 8am–4.45pm), which is also known as the Temple of 1,000 Lights because the 15m (50-ft) -high statue of the seated Buddha is surrounded by a halo with that many light bulbs. Inside the door is part of a branch from the sacred bodhi tree under which the Buddha is said to have attained enlightenment. Worshippers may illuminate the lights around the statue for a small donation.

### LEONG SAN SEE TEMPLE

Further down the road on your left are some lovely old houses and the **Leong San See Temple** ❾ (no. 371; daily 6am–6pm) with an ornately carved roof. The temple is dedicated to Guan Yin, the Goddess of Mercy. Its altar also has an image of Confucius; the temple is hence popular with parents who bring their children to pray for success in examinations.

Have a meal at one of the popular restaurants on Race Course Road, such as **Banana Leaf Apolo**, see ❸, before you call it a day. The Farrer Park MRT station is nearby.

## Food and drink

### ❶ ANANDA BHAVAN

58 Serangoon Road; tel: 6396 5464; www.anandabhavan.com; daily 7.30am–10pm; $
Established in 1924, Ananda Bhavan serves excellent South Indian vegetarian dishes, like crispy *thosai*, a pancake made of rice and gram flour.

### ❷ KOMALA VILAS

76–78 Serangoon Road; tel: 6293 6980; daily 7am–10:30pm; www.komalavilas.com.sg; $
This place is known for its cheap vegetarian Indian food and its many varieties of *thosai*.

### ❸ BANANA LEAF APOLO

54–58 Race Course Road; tel: 6293 8682; www.thebananaleafapolo.com; daily 11am–10.30pm; $$
The fish-head curry is a must-try, as is the mutton or chicken *biryani* (basmati rice cooked with spices), served on banana leaves.

# SENTOSA

*Sentosa, the largest of Singapore's offshore isles, is a recreational playground for everyone, with amusement rides and theme park–style attractions for families with children, and nice white-sand beaches for sun worshippers.*

**DISTANCE:** 4km (2.5 miles)
**TIME:** A full day, or overnight
**START:** Resorts World Sentosa
**END:** Wings of Time
**POINTS TO NOTE:** The fastest way to the island is to take the Sentosa Express light rail (daily 7am–midnight) from VivoCity mall Lobby L, Level 3 on the mainland. It takes less than 5 minutes to reach Imbiah Station. To get to VivoCity, take the MRT to HarbourFront Station. You can also get to Sentosa by taxi or cable car (tel: 6377 9688; www. onefabergroup.com; daily 8.45am– 10pm, last boarding 9.30pm). On the island, you can walk, or take the light rail or the free bus services and beach trams. Alternatively, you can get to the island on foot via the Sentosa Boardwalk. Stroll from VivoCity's waterfront promenade to Sentosa along a covered travellator (daily 7am–midnight).

**Sentosa** (www.sentosa.com.sg), located to the south of the main island, was once known as Pulau Blakang Mati ('the island at the back of death' in Malay) because of the frequent outbreaks of fatal disease. Before it was turned into a leisure playground and renamed Sentosa, which means 'the isle of peace and tranquillity' in Malay, it was at different times a refuge for pirates, a military garrison and a detention centre for citizens arrested under the Internal Security Act.

Today, Sentosa is filled with activities and attractions. It has something for everyone, from historical sights to laid-back beaches to child-centric attractions. It would be too exhausting to see all the attractions in a single day. This itinerary covers the highlights. If you are inspired to see more, stay overnight at one of the hotels or resorts (see page 111).

### Resorts World Sentosa
After an extensive redevelopment, Sentosa today is a must-visit spot, especially for families. The sprawling 'integrated resort' **Resorts World Sentosa ❶** (www.rwsentosa.com) boasts a

*Sentosa has an idyllic tropical setting*

casino, mid-range and upscale hotels and restaurants, as well as a slew of high-end boutiques. The biggest draw here is the Universal Studios theme park, the only one in Southeast Asia.

The nearest train stop is Waterfront Station. Hop off and have breakfast at **Toast Box**, see ①. Then head to **Universal Studios Singapore** (www.universalstudiossingapore.com; daily summer 10am–8pm, winter until 6pm, operating hours subject to change). You can spend an entire day exploring the seven zones and 24

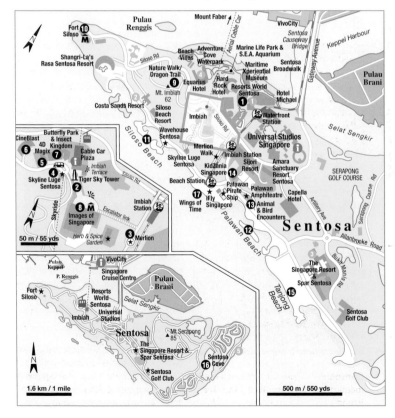

*Universal Studios*

attractions, of which 18 are exclusively designed for Singapore. Themed ride highlights include Shrek's 4-D Adventure, *Jurassic Park* Rapids Adventure, Madagascar's tropical jungle based on the DreamWorks movie, Ancient Egypt with the *Revenge of the Mummy* ride, and Transformers The Ride: The Ultimate 3D Battle. Online pre-booking is usually necessary, especially during the busy school holidays.

Other attractions include a Marine Life Park, touted as the world's largest oceanarium. You can easily spend an entire day here. Within the park is the S.E.A. Aquarium (daily 10am–7pm, hours may vary so check Resorts World Sentosa website), which has more than 800 species of marine animals and over 200 sharks. At the Adventure Cove Waterpark (daily 10am–6pm) you can snorkel with 20,000 tropical fish or float down Adventure River, passing through 14 themed zones. Over at the Maritime Experiential Museum, experience an interactive voyage along the ancient Maritime Silk Route and the 360-degree multi-sensor Typhoon Theatre.

## IMBIAH LOOKOUT

To enjoy great views of the Singapore harbour and the surrounding islands, there are two options close to Imbiah Station, though it's only worth ascending on clear days.

One is the 110m (360ft) **Tiger Sky Tower** ❷ (www.skytower.com.sg; daily 9am–9pm), whose lift whisks you up for a view from 131m (430ft) above sea level. The other is the 37m (120ft) **Merlion** ❸ (daily 10am–8pm), which is also the focus of a show with smoke and laser lights at night. Head across Merlion Plaza to the escalators to visit **Madame Tussauds Singapore** (Mon–Fri 10am–6pm, Sat–Sun 10am–7.30pm).

### Thrill rides

Kids and thrill-seekers will like the **Skyline Luge Sentosa** ❹ (www.skylineluge.com/en/sentosa; daily 10am–9.30pm). After buying your ticket at the booth near Beach Station, ascend a slope by way of a four-seater chairlift (Skyride) and whizz down a 650m/yd paved track in a luge, which is a cross between a go-kart and a toboggan.

Near the top of the Skyride is **Sentosa 4D Adventureland** ❺ (www.4dadventureland.com.sg; daily 10am–9pm, last show at 8.15pm), with an engaging 4D movie experience. More gripping action is to be found at the high-tech **Sentosa Cine-Blast** ❻ (daily 10am–9pm), located behind 4D Magix.

### Butterfly Park & Insect Kingdom

For something more subdued, stroll through the lush grounds of the **Butterfly Park & Insect King-**

*Sentosa CineBlast*

**dom** (www.jungle.com.sg; daily 9.30am–7pm), located next to Sentosa 4D Adventureland. As many as 1,500 butterflies from more than 50 species, including some endangered ones, flutter around in this conservatory. It is also home to over 3,000 species of insects.

### Images of Singapore
The best attraction in the Imbiah cluster is **Images of Singapore** (www.imagesofsingaporelive.com; Mon–Fri 11am–6pm, Sat–Sun 11am–7.30pm). Housed in a former military hospital, this museum has waxwork exhibits that recount Singapore's social history.

### Nature Walk
Nature lovers can explore the 1.5km (1-mile)-long **Nature Walk** , which starts from the Cable Car Arrival Plaza. Wander through a secondary rainforest and look out for vegetation such as the insectivorous pitcher plants and huge Tembusu trees.

## FORT SILOSO

At the western tip of the island you'll find one of Sentosa's must-sees, **Fort Siloso** (daily 10am–6pm). The fort's tunnels and guns were built in the 1880s for the defence of Singapore by the British. During World War II, the British pointed all their guns out to sea. This proved futile as the Japanese unexpectedly invaded overland from the north.

The armoury and cannons are still on display. The Surrender Chambers here bring to life Singapore's formal surrender to the Japanese in 1942 through a mix of gripping real audio-visual footage, artefacts and realistic wax figurines.

## BEACHES

Although the views are somewhat marred by container ships in the distance, Sentosa's beaches are probably Singapore's finest stretches of sand, running some 3km (2 miles) along the southern shore of the resort island and interspersed with scenic lagoons and coconut groves.

### Siloso Beach
**Siloso Beach** is a hotspot for watersports and beach volleyball. From here you can take to the sea on rental windsurfers, canoes and pedal boats, join bare-chested young men and bikini-clad ladies for a game of volleyball, or chill out at **Trapizza**, see , a nice spot for a cool beer and lunch.

Adventure-seekers can free-fall through the air at **iFly Singapore** (www.iflysingapore.com; Thu–Tue 9am–9.30pm, Wed 11am–9.30pm), the world's largest themed wind tunnel for indoor skydiving. This attraction is located beside the Beach

*Fort Siloso*

Station. About five minutes' walk from this station is **Wavehouse Sentosa** (www.wavehousesentosa.com; Mon–Fri 11.30am–9.30pm, Sat–Sun 10.30am–9.30pm). There, surfers, both novices and experts, can enjoy riding 10-foot man-made waves. After hanging up your wetsuit, you can sip cocktails, have a bite to eat and listen to live music.

*Palawan Beach*

Over at **Palawan Beach** ⑫, you can climb onto the **suspension bridge**, which links the main island to a tiny islet billed as the southernmost point of continental Asia. On the islet are two towers, clad in wood and bamboo, that afford a view of the sea.

The Palawan Beach area is increasingly being given over to family activities. Near the beach is the Palawan Amphitheatre, the venue of **Animal & Bird Encounters** ⑬ (daily shows 2–5.30pm), where the audience can snuggle up to snakes, primates and birds during performances. Those with little ones should also be sure to check out the **Palawan Pirate Ship** (10am–6pm; free), a couple of minutes' walk from here. Aimed at children aged 3–10, the Pirate Ship is a water play area with small water slides, spouting fountains and a swinging pirate's head.

**KidZania Singapore** ⑭ (www.kidzania.com.sg; daily 10am–6pm) is also located in the Palawan Beach area. At this interactive child-sized theme park, kids (aged 4–17) get to run a small fantasy town, play-acting in roles ranging from bank teller or firefighter to chicken shop owner. The city's functioning economy (and its currency, kidZos) helps little minds comprehend the concept of money.

*Tanjong Beach*

On the eastern side of Sentosa is **Tanjong Beach** ⑮, a more peaceful and secluded spot removed from the madding crowd, great for relaxing with a book and cool drink.

## SENTOSA COVE AND QUAYSIDE ISLE

At one edge of the island is **Sentosa Cove** ⑯, a posh residential area with multi-million dollar homes, and Quayside Isle, a dining enclave facing a marina filled with bobbing yachts. Well-heeled locals and expats frequent the many restaurants at the weekend. Right at the end of Quayside Isle is W Singapore hotel, which attracts the trendy set to its host of lively parties and events.

## EVENING ENTERTAINMENT

End the day at **Wings of Time** ⑰ (Siloso Beach; www.wingsoftime.com.sg; daily 7.40pm and 8.40pm), a multi-sensorial night show set in the open sea. Children will enjoy the contempo-

*The Wings of Time show*

*Sentosa has some fine beaches*

rary storyline showcasing multimedia effects including 3D projection mapping, state-of-the-art lasers, robotic water fountains, giant water jets and pyrotechnics.

Sentosa has no lack of dinner options, with a number of restaurants that are ranked among the best in Singapore.

Recommended are **The Cliff**, see ❸, **Forest**, see ❹ and **SKIRT**, see ❺.

Sentosa's chill-out spots are concentrated on the beaches. Over at Tanjong Beach, party-goers can sip cocktails and enjoy the sunset at Tanjong Beach Club (www.tanjongbeachclub.com).

## Food and drink

### ❶ TOAST BOX

26 Sentosa Gateway, Resorts World #B1-203/204; tel: 6686 3764; https://www.toastbox.com.sg; daily 6am–2am; $

Have a local breakfast of kaya toast, soft boiled eggs and freshly brewed coffee. For something more substantial, slurp up spicy noodles such as *laksa* and *mee siam*.

### ❷ TRAPIZZA

Siloso Beach; tel: 6376 2662; daily 11am–10pm; $$$

Trapizza, fresh from a recent revamp, is an Italian-style restaurant offering fine wood-fired pizzas, pastas and other casual fare. There is also a children's set menu, plus a water play area.

### ❸ THE CLIFF

Sofitel Singapore Sentosa Resort & Spa, 2 Bukit Manis Road; tel: 6708 8310; www.sofitel-singapore-sentosa.com/dining/the-cliff/; daily noon–3.30pm, 6–10pm, Fri–Sat until 10.30pm, Sat prosecco brunch noon–2.30pm; $$$$

Amid The Cliff's romantic setting by the sea, dine on the finest seafood as well as contemporary creations. There is also a good selection of French oysters.

### ❹ FOREST

8 Sentosa Gateway, Resorts World Sentosa, Level 1, Equarius Hotel; tel: 6577 6688; https://www.rwsentosa.com/en/restaurants/forest; daily 7.30–10.30am, noon–2.30pm and 6–10.30pm, Sun lunch until 3pm, $$$$

Modern Chinese restaurant by celebrity chef Sam Leong with a theatre kitchen where you can watch your meals being whipped up.

### ❺ SKIRT

21 Ocean Way; W Singapore – Sentosa Cove; tel: 6808 7278; http://www.skirt.wsingaporesentosacove.com; Sun–Thu 6–11.30pm, Fri–Sat 6pm–midnight, Sat also noon–3pm; $$$$

A vibrant dining experience awaits meat lovers at Skirt. The beef served here is aged in glass cabinets and the chefs fire up all meat cuts in the open kitchen right in the centre of the restaurant.

*Singapore Island Cruises*

# SOUTHERN ISLANDS

*Around Sentosa is a cluster of islets known as the Southern Islands, comprising Kusu, a place of rest and worship; St John's, a holiday spot with an easygoing air; and Sisters' Islands and Pulau Hantu, both of which are popular diving areas.*

---

**DISTANCE:** 13km (8 mile) round trip
**TIME:** Half a day
**START/END:** Marina South Pier
**POINTS TO NOTE:** To get to the Marina South Pier, take bus no. 402 from the Marina Bay MRT station.

---

A ferry service, which first stops at St John's Island followed by Kusu Island, is run by **Singapore Island Cruises** (tel: 6534 9339; www.islandcruise. com.sg). To get to Sisters' Islands or Pulau Hantu, charter a boat; this can also be organised through Singapore Island Cruises. Ferries depart from the Marina South Pier (see website for schedule).

## ST JOHN'S ISLAND

Situated approximately 6.5km (4 miles) south of Singapore, the 39-hectare (96-acre) **St John's Island** ❶ is a peaceful getaway with sandy beaches, lagoons, holiday bungalows and plenty of flora and fauna to gaze

upon. This was where Raffles' ship anchored before he met the Malay chief on Singapore island in 1819. St John's Island served as a quarantine centre for immigrants until the 1950s before it was used as a holding centre for political detainees.

## KUSU ISLAND

**Kusu** ❷, which means 'Tortoise Island' in the Chinese Hokkien dialect, is located about 6km (3.5 miles) south of the Singapore island. Legend has it that two shipwrecked sailors, Malay and Chinese, were saved by a tortoise that transformed itself into an island. Each man gave thanks and built a place of worship according to his own belief.

About 130,000 worshippers throng Kusu during the ninth lunar month of the calendar, usually between September and November. During other times of the year, the island is quieter. The island can be effortlessly covered on foot in less than an hour.

Day-trippers can enjoy a dip in the two lagoons, which are also good spots

*Tua Pek Kong temple on Kusu Island*

for picnicking. There are many shady trees and picnic tables as well as public toilets and showers. It is best to pack your own food and drinks for a picnic.

Overnight stays are not allowed on Kusu Island, so don't miss the last ferry back to Singapore island.

### Chinese Temple

The Taoist **Tua Pek Kong Temple** was actually built by a well-to-do merchant in 1923. It has classical Chinese green-tiled roofs and red walls and is reached via a series of pavilion-studded bridges set over a picturesque lagoon. Besides the Tua Pek Kong, the God of Prosperity, Guan Yin, the Goddess of Mercy, is also enshrined here. Also check out the **Tortoise Sanctuary**, which is home to hundreds of tortoises.

### Muslim shrines

Climb 152 steps to the summit of the hill. Standing here are three Muslim *keramat* (shrines), built to pay tribute to the devout Dato Syed Abdul Rahman, and his mother and sister, who lived in the early 19th century. These shrines are popular with childless couples who come to pray for fertility.

## PULAU HANTU AND SISTERS' ISLANDS

**Pulau Hantu** ❸ (Ghost Island), to the northwest of Sentosa, was so named because it was said to be haunted by the spirits of two ancient warriors who fought to their deaths here. Enveloped by coral reefs, it is regarded as one of Singapore's best diving spots.

Singapore's richest coral reefs line the coasts of the two isles (Palau Subar Darat and Palau Subar Laut) collectively known as **Sisters' Islands** ❹, which lie to the west of St John's Island. The currents can be pretty strong here, so be cautious when swimming.

*An Indian peacock at Jurong Bird Park*

# WESTERN SINGAPORE

*This part of the island has several attractions worth seeing, especially if you have kids in tow. The Jurong Bird Park and the Science Centre appeal to inquisitive minds, while Jurong Lake Gardens are set to offer quiet respite.*

**DISTANCE:** Varies
**TIME:** A full day
**START:** Jurong Bird Park
**END:** Singapore Science Centre
**POINTS TO NOTE:** These three attractions are not located near each other. To get to the bird park, take the MRT to the Boon Lay station and transfer to bus no. 194 or 251. A daily bus service (charge) goes from VivoCity and bus stops near some downtown hotels. To go on to the Science Centre, take a taxi or the MRT to Jurong East station and transfer to bus no. 335.

Western Singapore, although the country's industrial zone, has green spaces and a few family-friendly theme parks.

## JURONG BIRD PARK

The 20-hectare (49-acre) **Jurong Bird Park ❶** (2 Jurong Hill; www.birdpark.com. sg; daily 8.30am–6pm) is home to some 3,500 birds across 400 different species. The landscaped grounds make for a pleasant walk, and there are immersive walk-in aviaries. Be aware that the bird park is scheduled to move to a new location on Madal Lake Road in 2020.

Check the board for the show times and plan your route accordingly. Highly entertaining shows include Kings of the Skies (daily 10am and 4pm) and the High Flyers Show (daily 11am and 3pm).

As you walk in, you will see the **Penguin Coast** which houses six species of penguins. Other attractions include the **Parrot Paradise** with the park's most colourful and friendly residents and the **Pelican Cove**, where visitors can view underwater feeding of pelicans.

The **Wings of Asia Aviary** is a lush walk-through rainforest with the largest selection of birds in the park. Another outstanding attraction is the **Lory Loft**, a walk-in aviary hosting some 1,000 free-flying lories. From the elevated boardwalk you take in 360-degree views of the simulated Australian Outback.

Around the walk-in **Waterfall Aviary**, with the thunderous man-made **Jurong Falls**, birds originating from Africa and South America fly free.

Have a bite at **Hawk Café**, see ❶.

*Jurong Falls*                    *A parrot at a Jurong Bird Park show*

## JURONG LAKE GARDENS

A short taxi ride from the bird park is the **Jurong Lake**, chosen as the site for Singapore's newest national gardens, **Jurong Lake Gardens ❷** (free). The gardens will eventually comprise 90 hectares (222 acres) of green space across three sections: Jurong Lake Gardens West, Jurong Lake Gardens Central and Jurong Lake Gardens East. Waterfront areas will be landscaped for community activities, plus spaces for retail and food outlets. Jurong Lake Gardens West is scheduled to open in 2019, with the other two sections to follow from 2020.

The gardens will incorporate the existing **Chinese Garden** and **Japanese Garden**, which will receive a major upgrade. Landmark features, including the pagoda, tea house and bonsai garden, will remain.

### SCIENCE CENTRE

The nearby **Science Centre ❸** (15 Science Centre Road; www.science.edu.sg; daily 10am–6pm) has a mind-boggling 1,000 science exhibits.

Interesting exhibits on the social responsibility of science include the **Bioethic** and **Ecogarden** exhibits. Optical illusions are found in the **Mind's Eye Gallery**, and children will find the sculptures

and water features in the **Kinetic Garden** especially engaging. The adjacent **Omni-Theatre** screens IMAX movies. There's also a snow centre.

If you are hungry walk over to JEM mall with options such as **Din Tai Fung**, see ❷.

## Food and drink

### ❶ HAWK CAFÉ

Jurong Bird Park; tel: 6661 7858; Mon–Fri 8.30am–6pm, Sat–Sun 8am–6pm; $$
At the entrance of Jurong Bird Park, this pleasant eatery offers classic Singaporean dishes like *nasi lemak*.

### ❷ DIN TAI FUNG

50 Jurong Gateway Road, 02-07 JEM; tel: 6694 1161; www.dintaifung.com.sg; Mon–Fri 11am–9.30pm, Sat–Sun 10.30am–9.30pm; $$
This popular spot offers pork and vegetarian dumplings, steamed buns and noodles.

*Singapore city centre from Mount Faber*

# SOUTHERN SINGAPORE

*The summit of Mount Faber is an ideal spot to take in panoramic views of Singapore's harbour. After the sun has set, swing by VivoCity, the city's largest mall, for a shopping spree or a meal at one of its many eateries.*

**DISTANCE:** 1.5km (1 mile)
**TIME:** Half a day
**START:** Mount Faber
**END:** VivoCity
**POINTS TO NOTE:** Start this tour in the late afternoon. To ascend Mount Faber, take a taxi or the cable car.

Southern Singapore is most well known for the Port of Singapore and as the gateway to Sentosa (see page 78). Hike up Mount Faber to soak up the views and then descend to the city's largest shopping mall, VivoCity, at the foot of the hill.

## MOUNT FABER

**Mount Faber ❶** is a 110m (360ft) -high hill blanketed by one of the oldest rainforests in Singapore. Formerly called Telok Blangah

Hill, it was renamed in 1845 after Captain C.E. Faber of the Madras Engineers, who built the road up to the summit.

Exit the HarbourFront MRT station from Exit D to Marang Road. This road leads to the **Marang Trail**, with stairs and shaded footpaths weaving through a secondary forest. The walk takes 15 to 20 minutes. The Marang Trail connects to Faber

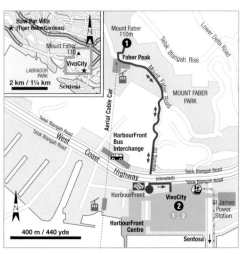

*In VivoCity*

Walk, leading to the cable car station and **Faber Peak Singapore** (www.onefaber group.com; daily 8.30am–10pm) on the summit. From here, enjoy splendid vistas, especially delightful at sunset. Have a pre-dinner drink and bites at **Moonstone**, a yakitori-sake bar. Retrace your steps down the hill (the Marang Trail is deliberately unlit after dark to minimise disturbance to nocturnal life, so bring a torch if you choose to take this trail). Otherwise, it is easier to call for a taxi. For something a little more dramatic, opt for a cable-car ride down to HarbourFront. Or, for a truly unique experience, book the Sky Dining experience where you can take in the views of the skyline while you dine in a cable car drifting between Mount Faber and Sentosa 70m (230ft) above the sea (reservations: tel: 6377 9688; www.one-fabergroup.com).

## VIVOCITY

Inspired by the waterside location, Japanese architect Toyo Ito created a fluid facade that evokes sea waves for **VivoCity** ❷ (1 Harbourfront Walk; tel: 6377 6860; www.vivocity.com.sg; daily 10am–10pm). It has hundreds of stores and restaurants; in fact this mall is so huge you will need more than half a day to cover it thoroughly. Browse at leisure or head to one of its many food and beverage outlets such as **The Queen and Mangosteen**, see ❶, or **TungLok Signatures**, see ❷.

---

## Haw Par Villa

Also known as Tiger Balm Gardens, Haw Par Villa (meaning 'villa of the tiger and the leopard') was named after its owners, the brothers behind the famous Tiger Balm ointment. Built in 1937, the park features grotesque statues that illustrate Chinese mythological stories and notorious crimes. When Boon Par died in 1945, Boon Haw turned it into a public park. New management took over in 2015, immediately getting to work to give the languishing park a facelift. To get to the park (262 Pasir Panjang Road; daily 9am–7pm; free), take bus no. 188 from the HarbourFront Bus Interchange or bus no. 200 from the Buona Vista MRT station.

---

## Food and drink

### ❶ THE QUEEN AND MANGOSTEEN
#01-106-107 VivoCity 1, Harbourfront Walk; tel: 6376 9380; Mon–Thu noon–midnight Fri–Sat until 1am, Sun 10am–midnight; $$
This British gourmet pub overlooks the waterfront and Sentosa Island and serves up decent pub grub.

### ❷ TUNGLOK SIGNATURES
01-57 VivoCity; tel: 6376 9555; www.tunglok.com; Mon–Sat 11.30am–3pm and 6–10.30pm, Sun 11am–3.30pm and 6–10.30pm; $$$
Cantonese, Shanghainese and Sichuan dishes woven with creativity.

*Ornate terrace houses on Koon Seng Road*

# KATONG AND THE EAST COAST

*Known for laid-back, beachside living, Katong in eastern Singapore is also a veritable living museum of Straits Chinese culture, with decades-old Peranakan eateries and floridly decorated conservation terrace houses.*

---

**DISTANCE:** 2km (1.25 miles), more if you want to explore the East Coast Park
**TIME:** A half/full day
**START:** Kuan Im Tng Temple
**END:** East Coast Park
**POINTS TO NOTE:** Take a short taxi ride from the Paya Lebar MRT station to Tembeling Road.

---

Katong is roughly bounded by Tanjong Katong Road, Mountbatten and East Coast roads, Changi Road and Telok Kurau Road. In the early 19th century, Katong was situated just by the sea. Portuguese and Chinese settlers planted cotton, coconut and gambier in the area, whose name was derived from a species of sea turtle that was once found in Singapore. After World War I, it became home to well-heeled Chinese, Peranakans and Eurasians. This area has long enjoyed a reputation for good food.

Due to land shortage in the 1970s, this area was reclaimed, all the way to the East Coast Parkway.

## JOO CHIAT

The first stop of the walk is **Kuan Im Tng Temple ❶** at no. 62 on Tembeling Road, which is parallel to Joo Chiat Road. This ornate temple, with dancing dragons adorning its roofs and pillars, was built in 1921. It is dedicated to Buddhism, Taoism and Confucianism, with the Jade Emperor, the Goddess of Mercy (Guan Yin), the God of War (Guan Di) and several other deities enshrined in the prayer hall. Note its courtyard wall of Chinese paintings, illustrating classic stories of filial piety.

## KOON SENG ROAD

Exit the temple and turn right on Tembeling Road. When you come to **Koon Seng Road ❷**, turn right. The row of prewar conservation terrace houses is a perfect showcase of the flamboyant Peranakan architectural style. Before World War II, many wealthy Peranakans built lavish homes that displayed a unique fusion of Chinese, Malay

*Sri Senpaga Vinayagar Temple*

and European design elements. Typically these houses are underscored by plasterwork with flora and fauna motifs and intricate tiles, and feature a pair of carved wooden *pintu pagar* ('fence doors').

Continue to Joo Chiat Road, where you can hire a taxi to get to the next stop, Ceylon Road. If you choose to go on foot, note that it will be a lengthy walk with not much to see except for bungalows and apartment blocks.

## ST HILDA'S CHURCH

At the junction of Ceylon and Fowlie roads stands the 1934 **St Hilda's Anglican Church** ❸ (41 Ceylon Road; http://sthildas.org.sg; daily 9am–6pm). Fashioned after an Eng-

lish parish church, the building is topped by a Victorian-style conical tower and features beautiful stained glass.

## SENPAGA TEMPLE

A 5-minute walk from St Hilda's Anglican Church is one of Singapore's oldest Hindu shrines, the **Sri Senpaga Vinayagar Temple** ❹ (19 Ceylon Road; daily 5.30am–12.30pm and 5.30–11pm). It dates back to the 1850s, when a statue of Lord Vinayagar, the Elephant God, was unearthed by the side of a pond. A Ceylonese (Sri Lankan) Tamil built the first temple structure, which was a simple shelter with a thatched *attap* (nipa) roof, positioned under a *senpaga* (Chempaka) tree. When the area was bombed during World War II, the main shrine remained intact. Today the temple, rebuilt in 1989, is an important place of worship for the Hindu community living in the east. It is noted for its 20m (65ft) -high *gopuram* (tower), above its entrance, which bears 159 sculptures of Hindu gods and deities.

## EAST COAST ROAD

After your temple visit, continue on Ceylon Road to **East Coast Road**.

### Peranakan culture

On East Coast Road, make sure to drop by **Kim Choo** (111 East Coast Road; www.kimchoo.com; daily

*Katong Antique House*

10am–10pm), a business started by Madam Lee Kim Choo in the late 1940s. She first learned her grandmother's secret recipe of making glutinous rice dumplings at the age of 12, and supported her four children by selling them. She has since handed over her thriving business to the next generation. Upstairs you will find a gallery, and Kim Choo's grandson, Raymond Wong, will gladly show you his collection of Peranakan artefacts, such as quality porcelain from Jiangxi, China, vintage batiks and intricate beaded slippers (he also offers a Peranakan beadworks workshop). One of the best souvenirs you can take away from here is a *sarong kebaya* (Nonya blouse and sarong skirt) with delicate embroidery. The boutique tour includes food sampling and a Peranakan shoe beading demonstration.

Just next door is **Rumah Bebe** ❺ (no. 113; www.rumahbebe. com; tel: 6247 8781; Tue–Sun 9.30am–6.30pm), a treasure trove of all things Peranakan, from furnishings and traditional apparel to jewellery and porcelain, housed in a 1928 shophouse. It is owned by former school teacher and renowned beadwork specialist Bebe Seet. Look out for the lovely bridal chamber on level two and the intricate *kasut manik manik*, dainty slippers of fine beadwork. Bebe also conducts bi-weekly beading classes to keep the craft, which is on the brink of vanishing, alive.

Another stop for Peranakan treats is **Glory Catering**, see ❶.

### Church of the Holy Family

East Coast Road is a long road. You can end your Katong tour after your meal, or explore a couple of other places along the stretch.

Generations of Peranakan and Eurasian Roman Catholics living in the east have worshipped at the **Church of the Holy Family** ❻ (6 Chapel Road; www.holyfamily.org.sg; daily 6am–7.30pm). In 1923, a chapel was built on this site only to be subsequently torn down in order to make way for this church, which was completed in 1932.

### Katong Antique House

Further down from the church is the **Katong Antique House** ❼ (208 East Coast Road, tel: 6345 8544; by appointment only), an iconic shop owned by Peter Wee. He is a fourth-generation Baba who began his business of buying, restoring and selling Peranakan furniture, porcelain and other cultural products in 1971. The shop is a treasure trove of traditional crockery, jewellery, beaded slippers, costumes and furniture. A small gallery sits on the upper level of the shophouse. Peter has in-depth knowledge of Peranakan heritage, so make an appointment if you want to be charmed by his fascinating stories of yore.

*Cycling in East Coast Park*

A few doors down from the antique shop is **328 Katong Laksa**, see ②, where you can enjoy the area's signature noodle dish. For something lighter, drop by **Chin Mee Chin**, see ③.

## EAST COAST PARK

Take a 5-minute taxi ride from East Coast Road to the **East Coast Park** ⑧ further south. The beach park, stretching about 20km (12 miles) between the Changi Airport and Marina Bay, is a popular recreational and dining destination.

The 7.5km (4.5-mile) reclaimed beach is unfortunately just narrow slopes of not-so-fine sand, and the waters are rather murky and not recommended for swimming. Locals, however, don't complain, as the balmy environment, with views of ships anchored in the Strait of Singapore, is refreshing after a week of toiling in air-conditioned offices. At the weekends, the park teems with picnicking families, joggers, campers, rollerbladers and cyclists. If you want to catch a glimpse of the Singaporeans at play, the park is a good place.

Like elsewhere in Singapore, the East Coast Park offers plenty to eat. The restaurants at the **East Coast Seafood Centre**, famed for Singapore-style seafood dishes like chilli and pepper crabs, are persistently booked out.

## Food and drink

### ① GLORY CATERING

139 East Coast Road; tel: 6344 1749; www. glorycatering.com.sg; Tue–Sun 8.30am–8.30pm; $–$$
An old-time favourite, well loved for its *nasi padang* (rice with Indonesian-style dishes) and Peranakan sweet treats, like pineapple tarts and coconut-milk-infused cookies and cakes.

### ② 328 KATONG LAKSA

216/218 East Coast Road; tel: 9732 8163; http://328katonglaksa.com; daily 10am–10pm; $
Many eateries in this area claim that they serve the best *laksa* (thick rice noodles in a rich, spicy coconut-milk-based gravy). 328 Katong Laksa is largely acknowledged as one of the best eatery options.

### ③ CHIN MEE CHIN

204 East Coast Road; tel: 6345 0419; Tue–Sun 8.30am–4pm; $
This bakery and coffee shop hasn't changed much since it opened more than sixty years ago. Loyal customers, spanning generations, keep coming here for coffee served in traditional porcelain cups, alongside soft-boiled eggs and *kaya* (coconut jam) toast. Traditional jam rolls, buns and cakes are popular for afternoon tea.

*The Changi Museum*

# CHANGI

*Peaceful Changi provides a welcome contrast to the frenzied city. Its star attraction is the poignant Changi Chapel and Museum, while laid-back Changi Village appeals with its restful and breezy atmosphere.*

**DISTANCE:** 5.5km (3.5 miles)
**TIME:** Half a day
**START:** Changi Chapel and Museum
**END:** Changi Beach Park
**POINTS TO NOTE:** Take a taxi to the Changi Museum or hop on bus no. 2 from the Tanah Merah MRT station. The bus stops opposite the museum. Note that the museum and chapel will be shut for restoration until late 2020. Take bus no. 2 from the same bus stop to Changi Village. To get to Pulau Ubin, walk to Changi Point Ferry Terminal (tel: 6542 7944), a few minutes from Changi Village Hawker Centre, and take a 10-minute bumboat ride (daily 6am–8pm; charge; boats leave when there are 12 passengers).

Changi is most well known as the location of Singapore's airport, but it also contains a few gems.

## CHANGI CHAPEL AND MUSEUM

During the Japanese Occupation from 1942 to 1945, the Japanese army turned the British-built barracks in Changi into a prisoner-of-war (POW) camp. It was a notorious hellhole where thousands of military and civilian prisoners were interned and endured appalling conditions and treatment.

Built in 1988, the **Changi Chapel and Museum ❶** (1000 Upper Changi Road North; www.changimuseum. sg; daily 9.30am–5pm; free) is dedicated to the POWs who were interned in Changi camp. The Chapel and Museum are both undergoing major

### Pulau Ubin

Located off Singapore's northeastern tip, Pulau Ubin (Granite Island) measures just 8km (5 miles) across and 1.5km (1 mile) wide. It is home to Singapore's last *kampung* (village), with about 100 villagers who still depend on well water and on diesel generators for electricity. Stop by the National Parks Board (NParks) information kiosk (daily 8.30am–5pm) to pick up a map and leaflets with details on the island's flora and fauna.

*Boats at Changi Point jetty*                    *The Changi Chapel*

redevelopment and are scheduled to re-open towards the end of 2020.

The **museum** provides moving insights into the POWs' lives in the Changi internment camp, which housed as many as 3,000 prisoners at one time. Among the exhibits are poignant letters, photographs, and personal effects donated by former POWs and their families, which portray the POWs' suffering and hope during those dark years. Especially notable are the sketches and paintings by William Haxworth and the photographs by George Aspinall.

### Changi Murals

The museum also features a replica of the Changi Murals. The Japanese military allowed a ward in the internment camp to be used as a chapel. Bombardier Stanley Warren, of the 15th Field Regiment, decorated the chapel with life-sized murals that depicted scenes from the life of Christ. These original murals, known as the **Changi Murals**, are now in the grounds of an operational military camp – Block 151 of Changi Airbase – and are open for public viewing only during four window periods in February, August, September and November. Visitors who wish to view them must apply at least two weeks ahead to the public relations department of the Ministry of Defence (24-hour hotline at 9228 6190). For many years after the war, the murals lay hidden and forgotten as the ward was used as a storage room, and were only discovered during renovations in 1958.

### Changi Chapel

The **Changi Chapel** is a replica of one of many similar places of worship erected by POWs while incarcerated in Changi

*Sunset at Changi Bay*

camp. The original chapel was dismantled after World War II and reassembled in Australia. This replica was built in 1988 in response to requests by former POWs and their families.

The chapel sits in a garden with hibiscus and frangipani plants. You are welcome to leave a flower on the altar or a note on a board to the left of the altar in remembrance of the POWs.

## CHANGI VILLAGE

When you are done, hop on a 10–15 minute bus or taxi ride to **Changi Village ❷**. Along the way you can see Changi Prison and various military sites behind barbed wire fencing.

When you reach Changi Village, head to the **hawker centre**, see ❶, for lunch, located next to the bus terminus.

Take time to wander around the sleepy village, a slice of charming old Singapore.

Seafood restaurants and pubs also line Netheravon Road, while the **Village Hotel Changi** (tel: 6379 7111; www.stayfareast.com) is among only a scattering of hotels in the area.

Changi Village is also home to a variety of splendid old trees. The magnificent *Shorea Gibbosa* tree, which has a cauliflower-like crown, at the junction of Netheravon and Turnhouse roads, is said to be one of the last two left in Singapore.

A short walk from the hawker centre is the **Changi Point Ferry Terminal**, where you depart on a bumboat to **Pulau Ubin**.

## CHANGI BEACH PARK

Take the footbridge to the 3km (2-mile)-long **Changi Beach Park ❸**. Changi Beach is a craggy stretch, so don't expect soft white sand under your feet. Higher tides can conceal sharp rocks; be careful and proceed slowly if you are wading in the water.

Still, the beach is popular with locals who come to picnic, fish on the pier, enjoy the sea breeze and watch planes land and take off from Changi Airport.

### Changi Massacre Site
Further east on Changi Beach is the **Changi Massacre Site ❹**, marked by a storyboard. This was where the sand was reported to have turned red with blood on 20 February 1942. Sixty-six Chinese men thought to be anti-Japanese sympathisers were lined up along the water's edge and killed by a Japanese firing squad.

---

## Food and drink

**❶ CHANGI VILLAGE HAWKER CENTRE**
01-08 Changi Village Market and Food Centre, 2 Changi Village Road; daily early morning till late; $–$$
Recommended are Wing Kee (01-04) for its *hor fun* (flat rice noodles) and International Muslim Food Stall (01-57) for its *nasi lemak*. But it is Charlie's Corner (01-08; tel: 6543 1754) that has been the favourite since the late 1970s, serving up excellent pub grub.

*Boardwalk through the rainforest*

# BUKIT TIMAH NATURE RESERVE

*A sanctuary containing one of Singapore's two virgin rainforests and a rich biodiversity, this reserve is easily accessed from the city centre. Hike up to the hilltop for panoramic views and spot tropical flora and fauna along the way.*

**DISTANCE:** 1km (0.6 mile)
**TIME:** 2–3 hours
**START/END:** Bukit Timah Nature Reserve Visitor Centre
**POINTS TO NOTE:** This is best as a morning excursion. Allow 30 minutes to get there from the city centre. From the Newton MRT station, bus no. 67, 170 or 171 takes you to Upper Bukit Timah Road. Alight at Bukit Timah Shopping Centre, cross Jalan Anak Bukit, walk up Hindhede Road and then to the end of Hindhede Drive. Going by taxi is by far the easiest way. Have the driver drop you off at the car park.

The **Bukit Timah Nature Reserve** (177 Hindhede Drive; tel: 6468 5736; www. nparks.gov.sg; daily 7am–7pm; free) is located almost in the geographic centre of Singapore, 12km (7.5 miles) from the city. It contains Singapore's highest hill, the **Bukit Timah Hill**, at 164m (538ft) above sea level, and offers 164 hectares (405 acres) of ecologically important lowland rainforest. The reserve underwent a two-year renovation between 2014 and 2016, and is looking better than ever.

## BACKGROUND

Most of Singapore's forest was heavily logged until the mid-19th century. In 1884, in response to research commissioned by the government of the Straits Settlements on climatic changes arising from deforestation, the Bukit Timah Nature Reserve was established. For more than a century, the forest was a botanical collecting ground.

The reserve has suffered significant changes in its biodiversity levels due to the poaching of animals and logging in the early 20th century and more recent urban encroachments. Large mammals like tigers and deer no longer roam the forest and ecologically rare birds like hornbills and trogons, once part of the virgin rainforest, have vanished.

Still, nature lovers will not go away disappointed. There are over 2,000 native plants and 170 species of ferns recorded. Soaring dipterocarp trees

are a feature of this reserve. Don't expect to find the plants that feature in Singapore's urban greenery, though, as most of those are imported species. This is Singapore as she was in her earliest days.

The wildlife impresses with its variety. There are some 2 million insects and invertebrates, 660 types of spiders and 126 species of birds. Small animals like squirrels, anteaters, treeshrews and long-tailed macaques have survived too, although are infrequently seen. Don't be tempted to feed the monkeys. The forest provides for them and they have been known to behave viciously.

## TRAILS

For your visit to Bukit Timah, wear comfortable clothing, sturdy shoes and scent-free insect repellent. The Visitor Centre (daily 8am–6pm) at the foot of the hill is a good place to start. Orientate yourself and check out the hiking routes clearly marked on the map at the entrance.

You can find maps and directional signs along the trails. You can get to the summit and back in under an hour, or you can spend up to 3 hours exploring more of the reserve – note that some of the paths can be muddy in wet weather.

The first part, straight up a paved road, can be disappointing, but once past this, you are in a primary rainforest complete with a heavy canopy at the uppermost layer, rattans and liana vines at mid-level, and red ginger flowers and dark purple bat lilies on the forest floor. On the summit, relish views of the surrounding rainforest and the **Seletar Reservoir** to the north.

On leaving Hindhede Drive, take a short taxi ride to the Rail Mall for lunch in at **Springleaf Prata Place**, see ❶.

## Food and drink

### ❶ SPRINGLEAF PRATA PLACE

The Rail Mall, 396 Upper Bukit Timah Road; tel: 6493 2404; www.springleafprataplace.com; daily 8am–midnight; $$
Try the soft, chewy *prata* with a variety of sweet or savoury dips like red bean, tomato, banana or pineapple, or opt for a more substantial chicken or mutton curry.

*At Singapore Zoo*

# MANDAI

*Lush Mandai is the setting of Singapore Zoo, where animals roam in naturalistic enclosures, and the one-of-a-kind Night Safari, where nocturnal wildlife prowls in the moonlight.*

**DISTANCE:** Varies
**TIME:** Half a day
**START:** Singapore Zoo
**END:** Night Safari
**POINTS TO NOTE:** Take either bus no. 138 from the Ang Mo Kio MRT station or bus no. 927 from the Choa Chu Kang MRT station. The two attractions are located next to each other on Mandai Lake Road. If you plan to visit the Singapore Zoo, River Safari and Night Safari, purchase the Park Hopper multi-park ticket at a discounted package price. Aim to arrive at the Singapore Zoo in the morning, followed by River Safari to look at the pandas and then head over to the Night Safari at 6pm.

The Singapore Zoo and the Night Safari, known to be among the most thoughtful zoo settings in the world, provide an experience that will appeal to all. The 'open concept' of both zoos allows animals to roam freely in naturalistic habitats. Visitors are separated from most of the animals only by water moats and other low barriers.

## SINGAPORE ZOO

The 26-hectare **Singapore Zoo** ❶ (www.zoo.com.sg; daily 8.30am–6pm) is nestled in a rainforest and displays some 2,800 animals representing 300 species, 29 percent of which are threatened. There is a lot to see at the zoo, so this route features just the highlights.

Before you begin, note the animal show and feeding times posted at the entrance, so you can plan your tour. Recommended animal shows are **Elephants at Work and Play**, which features these mammals moving logs, and **Splash Safari**, with antics by sea lions and jackass penguins. The most spectacular feedings are to be seen at the polar bear and lion enclosures. There is also a tram service (separate charge) that plies the zoo.

### Orangutans

The zoo has the world's largest colony of Bornean and Sumatran orangu-

*A fruit bat in the Fragile Forest*

tans, the result of a successful captive breeding programme. See these primates up close at two free-ranging areas. Here they hang out, literally and figuratively, among tall trees and swing across vines.

You can also have a **Jungle Breakfast with Wildlife** (daily 9–10.30am) in close proximity to orangutans as well as other creatures like snakes and otters at Ah Meng Restaurant (Terrace). Book via the website or tel: 6269 3411.

### Other highlights

Explore rainforest ecosystems in the **Fragile Forest**, a re-created tropical jungle that is a sanctuary to fauna as diverse as tamarins, lemurs, sloths, parakeets and butterflies.

Other themed areas worthy of your time include the **Great Rift Valley of Ethiopia**, where Hamadryas baboons dwell, the **Elephants of Asia**, reminiscent of the hills of Burma, and the **Australasia**, where kangaroos and wallabies prance around.

### Dinner and entertainment

After you are done with the zoo, move on to the Night Safari next door. For dinner, choose **Ulu Ulu Safari Restaurant**, see ❶. Another interesting dining option is the **Gourmet Safari Express** (tel: 6360 8560; daily 7–10pm), where you can dine and take in the animal exhibits at the same time in the comfort of a tram. Book at least one week ahead.

---

## River Safari

In 2013, the zoo's parent company, Wildlife Reserves Singapore, introduced River Safari (80 Mandai Lake Road; www.riversafari.com.sg; daily 10am–7pm), Asia's first and only river-themed wildlife park, and home to over 5,000 animals. Take a 'river adventure' down the Mississippi, Congo, Nile, Ganges, Murray, Mekong and Yangtze rivers, and visit the Squirrel Monkey Forest and Wild Amazonia. You can opt for a Reservoir Cruise (10.30am–6pm) or a ride on the Amazon River Quest (11am–6pm) to spot animals including the Brazilian tapir, jaguar and giant anteater. This park also houses the world's largest freshwater aquarium.

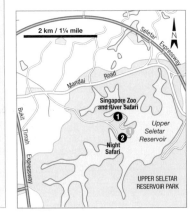

*Getting up close with a giraffe*

*Anteaters at the zoo*

## NIGHT SAFARI

If you have been disappointed with disinterested animals in day zoos, it could be because 90 percent of tropical mammals are active only at night. At the 40-hectare (99-acre) **Night Safari** ❷ (www.nightsafari.com.sg; daily 7.30pm–midnight), the first night zoo in the world, animals are seen at their most active, feeding, socialising and prowling. The 41 naturalistic habitats are unobtrusively lit with a gentle moonlight glow so that the animals are not disturbed. Some 2,500 animals representing 120 species, of which 29 percent are endangered, roam the Night Safari. The night zoo has also been successful in breeding endangered species such as the anteater, giant flying squirrel, Malayan flying fox and spotted hyena.

The Night Safari is extremely crowded at the weekend, so if you prefer a quieter visit, go on a weekday.

### Habitats

You can walk or travel around the seven geographical zones that replicate lands in Asia, Africa and South America. Visitors will find habitats such as the Nepalese river valley, Indian subcontinent, Himalayan foothills and African plains. The Night Safari features after-hours hunters such as tigers and lions, as well as lesser-known creatures like the Himalayan tahr mountain goat, babirusa

pig, one-horned rhino and barasingha swamp deer. It may not be a real safari, but it's probably the closest you can get to feeling you're in the wilderness. Free-ranging deer and other small animals wander to the tram, which makes a 45-minute journey around the park. As it moves along, your guide will point out the animals that come into view in a hushed tone. Flash photography harms the animals' eyesight in the long run and is therefore not allowed.

Not to be missed is the **Creatures of the Night** show featuring otters, civets and binturongs, while the **Thumbuakar Performance** is a fabulous fire show.

### Walking trails

You can hop off at designated points along the tram route to divert on foot along four shorter trails: the **Fishing Cat**, **Leopard**, **Wallaby** and **East Lodge Trail** where you can gaze upon the majestic Malaysian tigers. The trails are clearly marked and rangers are stationed along the way to guide you.

## Food and drink

### ⓵ ULU ULU SAFARI

Night Safari; tel: 6269 3411; daily 5.30–11pm; $$
Try local cuisine like satay, fish tikka and *mee goreng* (fried noodles) in an ethnic-inspired setting.

# DIRECTORY

Hand-picked hotels and restaurants to suit all budgets and tastes, organised by area, plus select nightlife listings, an alphabetical listing of practical information and an overview of the best books and films to give you a flavour of the city.

*Room at the Fairmont*

# ACCOMMODATION

Singapore has a range of accommodation from five-star hotels in the prime Marina Bay, Civic District and Orchard Road to smaller boutique hotels in atmospheric spots like Little India and Chinatown. The integrated resorts in Sentosa and Marina Bay have also been the forerunners to a whole range of luxury hotels, with many leisure activities on offer.

In terms of accommodation, amenities and service standards, Singapore's top-end hotels easily compare with the best in the world. Deluxe, first-class and business-oriented hotels have conference and business facilities, cable TV, IDD phones and high-speed internet access. No question, accommodation in Singapore is pricier than in some Southeast Asian cities, but there are many choices that suit all pockets.

An online hotel reservation system managed by the Singapore Hotel Association (SHA) can help you with last-minute bookings (www.stayinsingapore.com). The system provides real-time reservations and supplies instant confirmation. SHA also has reservation counters at the arrival halls in Changi Airport's Terminals 1, 2 and 3 to assist you with bookings. When booking directly with the hotel, always ask if they have promotional rates and if breakfast is included. And be aware that the standard 10 percent service charge and 7 percent Goods and Services Tax (GST) will add significantly to the final bill.

Price for a double room for one night without breakfast (not including the 10 percent service charge and 7 percent goods and services tax, except where noted):

$$$$ = over S$500
$$$ = S$350–500
$$ = S$150–350
$ = below S$150

## Civic District

### Carlton
76 Bras Basah Road; tel: 6338 8333; www.carltonhotel.sg; $$
This business-class hotel sits on a prime spot across from Chijmes and the Raffles Hotel. Choose from rooms in the Main Tower, Executive Wing or Premier Wing. Award-winning Cantonese restaurant and a bar and two cafés on site. A five-minute walk to the City Hall MRT station.

### Fairmont Singapore
80 Bras Basah Road; tel: 6339 7777; www.fairmont.com/singapore; $$$
Fairmont has 769 luxurious guest rooms and suites, with private balconies overlooking panoramic views

*A spacious Fairmont bathroom*

of the harbour or the cityscape. The hotel also offers a long list of amenities and excellent restaurants, including Szechuan Court and Mikuni. Its zen Willow Stream Spa is perfect for rejuvenating spa treatments. Conveniently located, with the City Hall MRT station literally on its doorstep.

### Hotel Fort Canning

11 Canning Walk; tel: 6559 6769; www. hfcsingapore.com; $$$

This colonial building was the British Far East Command Headquarters during World War II. Rooms are individually styled and there's also a gym, pool and Chinois Spa.

### Hangout@Mt.Emily

10A Upper Wilkie Road; tel: 6438 5588; www.hangouthotels.com; $$

This funky backpacker's lodging is about a 10-minute walk from the Dhoby Ghaut MRT station. Rooms are clean but small and with few frills. A great place to meet other travellers.

### Naumi

41 Seah Street; tel: 6403 6000; www. naumihotel.com; $$$

A chic 73-room boutique hotel, the Naumi offers plush designer comfort, a 50-inch plasma TV and kitchenette. An inviting rooftop infinity pool overlooks the city's skyline. The hotel's sixth floor is for ladies only. The City Hall MRT station is a convenient five-minute walk away.

### Raffles

1 Beach Road; tel: 6337 1886; www. raffles.com/singapore; $$$$

The Grand Dame of historical hotels, thoughtfully restored in 2018–19. Guests stay in suites and are cocooned in a private, genteel world, whilst gazing at museum-quality art pieces. The private pool is open 24 hours and bathrooms are designed for absolute indulgence. Across the road is the City Hall MRT station.

### Swissôtel The Stamford

2 Stamford Road; tel: 6338 8585; www. swissotel.com; $$$

Once the world's tallest hotel until it was supplanted in 1999, this hotel sits above the City Hall MRT station and is practically part of a large shopping centre complex. There is a business centre, convention centre and a huge number of restaurants and bars (including the rooftop Equinox complex with fine dining Jaan restaurant), plus a luxurious spa and a well-equipped fitness centre.

### Marina Bay

### Conrad Centennial

2 Temasek Boulevard; tel: 6334 8888; www.conradhotels.com; $$$

This five-star has spacious and luxurious rooms with picturesque views of Marina Bay. It is an excellent choice for business travellers with its wide range of facilities and fine restaurants such as Golden Peony and Oscar's.

The service staff are highly efficient. Convenient location for shopping, and only five minutes' walk to the Promenade MRT station.

## The Fullerton
1 Fullerton Square; tel: 6733 8388; www.fullertonhotel.com; $$$

Formerly the General Post Office, this historical jewel is now a luxury hotel. The colonnaded exterior gives way to a contemporary chic interior filled with Art Deco furniture. Amazing views from the 400 rooms and suites which either overlook the sunlit atrium courtyard, or have balconies that open out to panoramas of the city skyline, river promenade or Marina Bay. Raffles Place MRT station is five minutes away.

## Fullerton Bay Hotel
80 Collyer Quay; tel: 6333 8388; www.fullertonhotels.com/the-fullerton-bay-hotel; $$$$

An elegant hotel in a historic location that boasts stunning views of the Singapore skyline and bay. Exquisite touches include double-glazed floor-to-ceiling windows and Nespresso machines in all rooms. Have a meal at Clifford Pier followed by a nightcap at the Lantern rooftop bar. Within walking distance of Raffles Place MRT.

## Mandarin Oriental
5 Raffles Avenue; tel: 6338 0066; www.mandarinoriental.com; $$$

Its plush rooms have floor-to-ceiling windows that overlook the city. It's well known for its eateries: Morton's, The Steakhouse, Cherry Garden Cantonese restaurant and the pool-side, Mediterranean-style Dolce Vita restaurant. The Promenade MRT station is five minutes' walk away.

## Marina Bay Sands
10 Bayfront Avenue; tel: 6688 8868; www.marinabaysands.com; $$$

Located in the massive Marina Bay Sands integrated resort, this hotel overlooks the city centre and bay area. Pick from nine types of rooms and suites. Among the many facilities in the complex are a stunning infinity pool, casino and shops, as well as trendy bars and clubs.

## Marina Mandarin
6 Raffles Boulevard; tel: 6845 1000; www.meritushotels.com; $$$

Apart from its spectacular atrium rising through 21 storeys, all rooms offer breathtaking views of Marina Bay, while premier rooms and suites are equipped with plasma TVs. The hotel's fine restaurants include Peach Blossoms for Chinese food and Aqua-Marine for Asian and international cuisine. Only a short walk to the Esplanade MRT station.

## Pan Pacific Singapore
7 Raffles Boulevard; tel: 6336 8111; www.panpacific.com/singapore; $$$

*Sol LeWitt artwork adorns the atrium of Marina Bay Sands*

This hotel's 790 rooms and suites are contemporary and elegant, replete with beautiful views of the city or Marina Bay. It was the first hotel in Singapore to offer Wi-fi-operated mini-bars. Indian, Japanese and Chinese cuisines are available at its fine dining restaurants. The Promenade MRT station is a short walk away.

### Ritz-Carlton Millenia
7 Raffles Avenue; tel: 6337 8888; www.ritzcarlton.com/en/hotels/singapore#Hotel; $$$$

The sheer luxury hits you the moment you step into the foyer, with the contemporary design and marble-clad spaces studded with Dale Chihuly glass sculptures. Rooms are equally opulent but the pièce de résistance must surely be the oversized bathrooms with huge picture windows framing the large bathtubs. A less than five-minute walk to the Promenade MRT station.

### Westin Singapore
12 Marina View, Asia Square Tower 2; tel 6922 6888; www.westin.com/singapore; $$$

Take a lift up to the level 32 of Westin Singapore and you will find the island's highest hotel lobby. Occupying levels 32 to 46 of the Asia Square Tower 2 at Marina Bay, this is Singapore's first integrated hotel situated within an office building. The hotel rooms promises dazzling views of the sea and the bay. Sink into the signature Heavenly Bed with its patented pillow-top mattress for a good night's sleep. To relax, take a dip in the infinity pool followed by a treatment at the Heavenly Spa by Westin™.

## Singapore River

### Grand Copthorne Waterfront
392 Havelock Road; tel: 6733 0880; www.grandcopthorne.com.sg; $$–$$$$

The 550 rooms are nicely appointed and come with all the mod cons. The hotel also offers a long-stay option; La Residenza on the fifth and sixth floors comprises 24 luxurious studios, one- and two-bedroom units which come with kitchenettes. The hotel lobby has a buffet with interactive show kitchens.

## Chinatown

### Dorsett Singapore
333 New Bridge Road; tel: 6678 8333; www.dorsetthotels.com/singapore; $$

Located above Outram Park MRT interchange station, guests can explore Chinatown and the surrounding areas easily and enjoy plenty of food and drink options in the vicinity. Rooms are modern and equipped with Wi-Fi and Posturepedic mattresses. There's a landscaped roof garden and outdoor Jacuzzi to take a respite after all the sightseeing.

### Link
50 Tiong Bahru Road; tel: 6622 8585; www.linkhotel.com.sg; $$

The Link Hotel, last renovated in 2015, has clean and stylish rooms. The hotel's pre-war buildings, the Lotus and Orchid blocks, are connected by a unique bridge that spans across the bustling Tiong Bahru Road.

## Parkroyal on Pickering

3 Upper Pickering Street; tel: 6809 8888; www.parkroyalhotels.com; $$$

This stunning contemporary hotel houses a luxurious spa, infinity pool and poolside cabanas, sprawling sky gardens and even a jogging track high above street level. The rooms, decked out in natural elements, offer views of the river and city.

## The Scarlet

33 Erskine Road; tel: 6511 3333; www. thescarlethotels.com/singapore; $$

Located near Ann Siang Hill and Club Street, this 80-room boutique hotel is full of character. Its unabashedly gaudy interior is decked out in bold colours, and its five custom-designed suites each showcase a different look. The hotel boasts a gym, an open-air jacuzzi and a chic roof-top alfresco bar and restaurant overlooking Chinatown. Chinatown MRT station is a 10-minute walk away.

## Orchard Road

## Four Seasons

190 Orchard Boulevard; tel: 6734 1110; www.fourseasons.com/singapore; $$$$

An intimate and elegant property with a marbled foyer, plush furnishings and exquisite artworks – about 1,500 Asian and international art pieces are on display. All rooms feature custom-designed beds, marble bathrooms with double vanity basins, deep-soaking tubs and luxuries such as Italian cotton bathrobes and Japanese yukatas. It is only a five-minute walk to the Orchard MRT station.

## Goodwood Park

22 Scotts Road; tel: 6737 7411; www. goodwoodparkhotel.com; $$$

This grand and graceful landmark exudes a strong colonial-era charm, with landscaped gardens that add a touch of serenity to the bustle of Orchard Road. It has 233 tastefully appointed rooms and suites complete with modern amenities, two outdoor swimming pools, a gym and five excellent restaurants, a deli and a bar. The Orchard MRT station is a three-minute walk away.

## Grand Hyatt

10 Scotts Road; tel: 6738 1234; www. singapore.grand.hyatt.com; $$$$

A stone's throw from the Orchard MRT station, the Grand Hyatt impresses with its minimalist, almost stark decor and excellent service. The Grand Wing rooms are particularly lavish with soft linens and Bang & Olufsen sound systems. Dine at mezza9, where Sunday champagne brunch is a must.

*Goodwood Park's pool*

## Grand Park Orchard

270 Orchard Road; tel: 6603 8888; www.parkhotelgroup.com/orchard; $$

The hotel's location right in the middle of Orchard Road is highly convenient for shopaholics. The striking 'herring-bone' design featured on its exterior glass facade is echoed throughout the hotel including the stylishly designed rooms.

## Hilton Singapore

581 Orchard Road; tel: 6737 2233; www3.hilton.com; $$$

The city's longest-operating 5-star hotel, with a shopping arcade hous-ing international fashion boutiques. Also conveniently located near shop-ping malls and 5 to 7 minutes' walk from Orchard MRT station. Six dining options to choose from.

## Hotel Jen Orchardgateway

277 Orchard Road; tel: 6708 8888; www.hoteljen.com; $$

Part of the Shangri-La group, this four-star hotel located above Som-erset MRT offers comfort and value. After your shopping spree, head to the rooftop leisure, wading or lap pool and enjoy superb city views. Food-wise, there's a restaurant serving local and international fare, as well as an on-the-go deli counter.

## Mandarin Orchard Singapore

333 Orchard Road; tel: 6737 4411; www.meritushotels.com; $$$

With a fantastic location on Orchard Road, this swanky hotel offers 1,077 tastefully refurbished rooms and suites featuring in-room amenities such as flatscreen TVs, free in-house movies, a smartphone for free local and international calls and electronic safe. Dining options include the two Michelin-star Shisen Hanten. Two MRT stations (Orchard and Somerset) are within walking distance.

## Marriott Tang Plaza

320 Orchard Road; tel: 6735 5800; www.singaporemarriott.com; $$$

*Grand Hyatt lobby*

The pagoda-roofed hotel at the corner of Scotts and Orchard roads is a well-known landmark with the Orchard MRT station at its doorstep. Its location is perfect for shopping and nightlife. There is a popular alfresco café, a Cantonese restaurant and a poolside grill, among other eateries. The famous Tangs department store shares the same building.

### The Regent
1 Cuscaden Road; tel: 6733 8888; www.regenthotels.com; $$$
Expect spacious, well-appointed rooms and efficient service. It has an excellent Italian restaurant by the pool and fine dining Cantonese restaurant. Tanglin Mall is just next door and Orchard MRT station is a good 12-minute walk away.

### Royal Plaza on Scotts
25 Scotts Road; tel: 6737 7966; www.royalplaza.com.sg; $$$
Located on Scotts Road (near Orchard Road MRT station), this hotel offers tastefully decorated contemporary rooms with generous work spaces and a complimentary in-room minibar, which is replenished daily. Its lobby café, Carousel, features an international buffet spread and a gourmet deli filled with sweet treats.

### St Regis
29 Tanglin Road; tel: 6506 6888; www.stregis.com; $$$$

St Regis brings its trademark style to a prime spot on Orchard Road. The design and furnishings are a bit over the top, but no one can fault its stupendous range of facilities: pool-side Italian restaurant, fine dining Cantonese, French brasserie, spa, swimming pool, business centre, private butlers for every room and a fleet of Bentleys to chauffeur guests around. The Orchard Road MRT station is a 10-minute walk away.

## Little India

### Moon @ 23 Dickson
23 Dickson Road; tel: 6827 6666; www.moon.com.sg; $$
This is a no-fuss boutique hotel that's trendy, compact and comfortable. It's also close to Bugis MRT station, thus making it very convenient to get to any part of the city.

### Parkroyal on Kitchener Road
181 Kitchener Road; tel: 6428 3000; www.parkroyalhotels.com; $$
An excellent-value hotel near Serangoon Road, next to the Farrer Park MRT station and opposite the 24-hour Mustafa Centre. The rooms are spacious and feature modern comforts. Facilities include a café serving Asian and Western food, a Cantonese restaurant, a fitness centre and swimming pool.

### Wanderlust Hotel
2 Dickson Road; tel: 6396 3322; http://wanderlusthotel.com; $$

Housed in an old school built in the 1920s, the concept of this hotel is incredibly unique. Each of the four levels was designed by award-winning local design agencies. The rooms are quirky and fun, albeit rather small. Its wine and bistro bar features labels from boutique wineries.

## Sentosa

### Hard Rock Hotel Singapore

8 Sentosa Gateway, Sentosa Island; tel: 6577 8899; www.rwsentosa.com/en/hotels/hard-rock-hotel-singapore; $$$

Live it up like a rock star and get the legendary entertainment experience. Located within the Resorts World Sentosa integrated resort, it's ideal for visiting Universal Studios and exploring the rest of the island during your stay.

### Le Méridien Singapore

23 Beach View; tel: 6818 3388; www.lemeridiensingaporesentosa.com; $$$

This hotel is housed in a beautifully restored colonial building dating back to the 1940s. The hotel's World of Whisky lounge boasts a massive whisky collection. With the Imbiah Station (Sentosa Express) just opposite the hotel, guests can zip off to VivoCity in barely five minutes.

### The Singapore Resort & Spa Sentosa

2 Bukit Manis Road; tel: 6708 8310; www.sofitel-singapore-sentosa.com; $$$

Stunning resort-style hotel located on a forested hill. Features both hotel-style rooms and suites as well as villas with private pools. Linked by a path directly to the beach. You may just want to park yourself at this idyllic retreat and not venture into the city. Be sure to book a massage at its adjacent So Spa, set amongst lush gardens.

### Shangri-La's Rasa Sentosa Resort & Spa

101 Siloso Road; tel: 6275 0100; www.shangri-la.com; $$$$

Superb guest-rooms (454 of them) and facilities. Not the most convenient place to stay for easy access to the city, but instead, the resort offers extensive recreational activities, from sailing to cycling. Restaurants here include the Silver Shell Café, Trapizza and 8 Noodles, serving Mediterranean dishes and Asian-inspired specialities.

### W Singapore – Sentosa Cove

21 Ocean Way; tel: 6808 7288; www.wsingaporesentosacove.com; $$$

Located next to Sentosa Cove's Quayside Isle, this trendy hotel attracts those who want to get away from the city. Partygoers will like the energetic vibe. Aside from the plush rooms, it has a modern grill restaurant, an international restaurant, a lobby bar and pool deck.

*True Blue Cuisine*

# RESTAURANTS

Singapore's cultural diversity has given the island-state an explosion of flavours – Chinese, Malay, Indian and Peranakan – that is entirely its own. Add to this the world's major cuisines, and you have a city that is permanently feasting.

There are few places in the world where life revolves around food like it does in Singapore. Singaporeans talk about food all the time. People from all walks of life can debate on where to get the freshest seafood or the best chicken rice for hours on end – preferably over a meal.

The racial mix of Chinese, Malays and Indians, as well as an expatriate population from the world over, has led to a range of cuisines. These immigrants brought their favourite dishes, ingredients and techniques, resulting in a variety of unique creations that are available today in venues ranging from hawker stalls to world-class restaurants.

It's also common to see Singaporeans making a beeline for buffets. Some of the best ones are located in upscale hotels; they serve a superb mix of international favourites including decadent desserts and cheese. Especially popular among expats is Sunday brunch with free-flowing champagne and luxurious foods such as oysters and lobsters.

Lately, fine dining has been undergoing a transformation of sorts, with restaurants offering more casual concepts such as grills, bistros and tapas, yet still featuring high-quality seasonal ingredients and fine techniques. The city has continued to attract many world-class chefs, boosting Singapore's reputation as an energetic gastronomic city, including celebrity chefs from Tokyo, Paris and New York. High-profile names such as Joel Robuchon, Tetsuya, Mario Batali, Gordon Ramsey and Daniel Boulud have all opened restaurants in Singapore thanks to the opening of the two integrated resorts, Marina Bay Sands and Resorts World Sentosa, in 2010. The island has embraced these culinary heavyweights with open arms.

## Civic District

### Garibaldi

36 Purvis Street, 01-02; tel: 6837 1468; www.garibaldi.com.sg; daily noon–2.30pm, 6.30–10.30pm; $$$$

Garibaldi is synonymous with Italian fine dining in the city. Helmed by well-known Chef Roberto Galetti, the kitchen uses only the best seasonal ingredients from Italy. His specialities include fresh seasonal seafood pasta and a variety of robust risottos.

> Price guide for a meal for one (excluding drinks and taxes):
> $$$$ = over S$60
> $$$ = S$40–60
> $$ = S$20–40
> $ = below S$20

*Seafood and vegetable platter*

*DB Bistro Moderne's interior*

## Kopi Tiam

2 Stamford Road, 2/F, Swissôtel The Stamford; tel: 6431 6156; www.swissotel.com/hotels/singapore-stamford/dining; Mon–Fri 6–10am, 11.30am–2.30pm, Sat–Sun 6–11am, noon–2.30pm, Mon–Sun 6–10.30pm; $$$

Make a beeline for tasty local dishes such as the Hainanese chicken rice, *rojak* and *laksa*. Get your spice fix with the collection of special curries such as Devil's curry, Vindaloo and Malay curry.

## Mikuni

Level 3, Fairmont Singapore, 80 Bras Basah Road; tel: 6431 6156; www.fairmont.com/singapore/dining/mikuni; Mon–Sat noon–2.30pm, 6.30–10.30pm; $$$$

Choose to sit at the teppanyaki, sushi or robatayaki counters where you can watch the chefs in action. Otherwise, opt for the main dining area where you can feast on the highly creative kaiseki menu featuring the best seasonal produce. The lunch bento sets are just as exquisite.

## Shinji

Carlton Hotel, 76 Bras Basah Road; tel: 63386131; www.shinjibykanesaka.com; Mon–Sat noon–3pm, 6–10.30pm; $$$$

This is the first outpost of two-Michelin-starred chef Shinji Kanesaka's famous Edomae-style sushi restaurant in Tokyo. Exquisite menus of perfectly executed sushi and pristine seafood are served. Watch the chefs prepare them right in front of you at the counter seats.

## True Blue Cuisine

47/49 Armenian Street; tel: 6440 0449; www.truebluecuisine.com; Tue–Sat 11.30am–2.30pm, 5.30–9.30pm; $$$

Located close to the Peranakan Museum, this eatery is adorned with the owner Benjamin Seck's personal collection of Peranakan antiques and artefacts. The dishes are just as impressive, but portions are small. Try the spicy beef *rendang* and *ayam buah keluak* (chicken stewed with black nuts).

## Yhingthai Palace

36 Purvis Street; tel: 6337 1161; www.yhingthai.com.sg; daily 11.30am–2pm, 6–10pm; $$

This restaurant serves delightfully robust Thai cuisine. Must-tries include the papaya salad, deep-fried fish with mango sauce, string beans with shrimp, and for dessert, mango with sticky rice.

## Marina Bay

### DB Bistro Moderne

2 Bayfront Avenue, #B1-48 The Shoppes at Marina Bay Sands; tel: 6688 8525; www.dbbistro.com/singapore/; Mon–Fri noon–5pm, Mon and Sun 5.30–10pm, Tue–Sat 5.30–11pm, Sat–Sun 11am–5.30pm; $$$$

This contemporary American French bistro, helmed by celebrity chef Daniel Boulud, serves robust French fare created with flair. Its charcuterie and famous DB burger are must-tries. Brunch is served on weekends and a pre-theatre menu is available from 5.30pm to 7pm daily.

*Pizza at Pizzeria Mozza*

## Hai Tien Lo

7 Raffles Blvd; 3/F, Pan Pacific Singapore; tel: 6826 8240; www.panpacific.com; daily 11.30am–2.30pm, 6.30–10.30pm; $$$

This fine Cantonese restaurant serves elegant seafood dishes as well as its signature barbecued duck. A dim sum lunch buffet is available on weekdays with a mixed lunch buffet available on weekends.

## The Lighthouse

Level 8, The Fullerton Hotel, 1 Fullerton Square; tel: 6877 8911; www.fullertonhotel.com; daily noon–2.30pm, 6.30–10.30pm; $$$$

This small restaurant presents a fabulous fine dining Italian experience with stunning views. A great venue for romantic nights or special occasions. Well-executed Southern Italian cuisine covers dishes from regions like Campania, Sardinia and Sicily. The wine list is excellent too.

## Majestic Restaurant

5 Straits View, 04–01 Marina One, The Heart (East Tower); tel: 6250 1988; http://restaurantmajestic.com; daily 11.30am–3pm, 5.45–10pm; $$$$

This stylish modern Cantonese cuisine offers signatures such as a combination of wasabi prawn, Peking duck and pan-seared foie gras as well as grilled rack of lamb with Chinese honey.

## Pizzeria Mozza

10 Bayfront Avenue, #B1-42/46 The Shoppes at Marina Bay Sands; tel: 6688 8522; www.pizzeriamozza.com; daily noon–11pm; $$$

Pizzeria Mozza (adjacent to the finer Osteria Mozza) is celebrity chef Mario Batali's first venture into Asia. Mirroring his restaurant in California, this pizza joint filled with blaring rock music is lively and casual. There are two wood-burning ovens that churn out the most delicious pizzas in town.

## Rang Mahal

3/F, Pan Pacific Hotel, 7 Raffles Boulevard; tel: 6333 1788; www.rangmahal.com.sg; daily noon–2.30pm, 6.30–10.30pm; $$$$

This elegant restaurant has been serving top-class Indian cuisine from the northern, southern and coastal regions since 1971. Dine on beautifully plated hot stone tandoori lamb chops or tandoor-grilled Portobello mushrooms with spices. A gourmet lunch buffet is available from Sunday to Friday.

## Summer Pavilion

7 Raffles Ave; The Ritz-Carlton, Millenia; tel: 6434 5286; www.ritzcarlton.com/en/Properties/Singapore/Dining; daily 11.30am–2.30pm, 6.30–10.30pm; $$$

Flanked by a lush Chinese garden, Summer Pavilion is like a breath of fresh air. Feast on refined Cantonese dishes such as barbecued duck, fish noodles and flawlessly made dim sum.

## Waku Ghin

Marina Bay Sands, 10 Bayfront Avenue, Level 1; tel: 6688 8507; www.marinabaysands.

*Waku Ghin*                    *An elaborate sea urchin dish*

com/restaurants/waku-ghin; daily 5.30pm–
10.30pm; $$$$

This is renowned chef Tetsuya Wakuda's first restaurant outside of Sydney. Enjoy top-notch European cuisine with Japanese influence prepared with the freshest seasonal ingredients. The experience is highly personalised as you can talk to the chefs and watch them prepare your degustation meal right in front of you.

## Singapore River

### Ellenborough Market Café

Swissotel Merchant Court Hotel, 20 Merchant Road; tel: 6239 1848; www.swissotel.com/hotels/singapore-merchant-court/dining/ellenborough-market-cafe; daily 6.30am–10.30pm, noon–2.30pm, 6.30–10pm, high tea 3.30–5.30pm; $$$

Overlooking the Singapore River, this restaurant is especially popular among locals who love the buffet spread of international and local favourites. Dine on chicken curry, satay, laksa, sushi and sashimi, then finish off with a plethora of desserts like coconut-based cendol and assorted Nonya cakes.

### Kinara

57 Boat Quay; tel: 6533 0412; www.thekinaragroup.com; daily 11.30am–2.30pm, 5.30–10.30pm, with exceptions; $$

Dine by the Singapore River in a beautiful space decorated with antique furniture from Rajasthan. Warm, friendly staff serve cuisine from the North West frontiers of India. The signature roasted leg of lamb, marinated for over 24 hours, is a must-try.

### Local Princess Terrace

403 Havelock Road, Lobby Level, Copthorne King's Hotel; tel: 6318 3168; www.millenniumhotels.com.sg; daily 6–10.30am, noon–2.30pm, 6.30–10pm; $$

The Princess Terrace's is most famous for its authentic Penang-style buffet. Expect favourites such as *char kway teow* (flat rice noodles fried in sweet soy sauce), chicken curry, and delicious multi-coloured *Nonya* desserts – all prepared by experienced chefs from Penang.

## Chinatown

### Bar-Roque Grill

165 Tanjong Pagar Road, 01-00; tel: 6444 9672; www.bar-roque.com.sg; Mon–Fri noon–2.30pm, 6–10.30pm, Sat 6–10.30pm; $$$$

Alsace-born Chef Stephane Istel set up this convivial restaurant and bar at the corner of Amara Hotel. Check out the massive rotisserie that churns out all kinds of delicious meats such as juicy free-range chicken and hefty pork knuckle.

### The Blue Ginger

97 Tanjong Pagar Road; tel: 6222 3928; www.theblueginger.com; daily noon–3pm, 6.30–10.30pm; $$

This authentic Peranakan restaurant has been around for more than 10 years, satisfying customers with tasty offerings such as *ayam buah keluak* (stewed chicken with black nuts), beef *rendang* (dry beef curry) and the must-have, durian *cendol* (a dessert with green jelly).

*Cha kuay teow*

## Buko Nero

126 Tanjong Pagar Road; tel: 6324 6225; https://bukonero.com.sg; Thu–Sat noon–3pm, Tue–Sat 6.30–11.30pm; $$$-$$$$

The menu reflects an Italian-Asian marriage – Venice-born Oscar Pasinato cooks while his Singaporean wife Tracy serves – with signatures such as tofu and vegetable tower, spaghetti with spicy crabmeat and prawns, and Horlicks ice cream. The tiny no-frills seven-table restaurant is always full. Call at least two weeks ahead for dinner reservations.

## Gavroche

66 Tras Street; tel: 6225 8266; www.brasseriegavroche.com; Mon–Fri 11.30am–2.30pm, 6.30–10pm, Sat 6.30–10.30pm; $$$$

Located in a charming conservation shophouse, Gavroche is reminiscent of a typical Parisian brasserie. In fact, all the antique furnishings, including the bar, were hand-picked and shipped in from France. Chef Frédéric Collin showcases his grandfather's recipes in his classic French menu.

## Sabio

5 Duxton Hill; tel: 6690 7562; www.dhm.com.sg/sabio; Mon–Thu noon–11.30pm, Fri noon–midnight, Sat 5pm–midnight, Sun 11.30am–10.30pm; $$$

This tapas bar serves authentic Spanish bites, oysters, sangria and wine. Head there early as it gets busy in the evenings, plus the bar subscribes to a no reservations policy.

## Spizza for Friends

269 Jalan Kayu; tel: 6481 2453; www.spizza.sg; daily Mon–Fri noon–2.30pm, 6–10.30pm, Sat–Sun noon–10.30pm; $$

Spizza's winning formula: ingredients imported from Italy, a thin and crispy crust and a wood-fired oven. Try the Quinta Pizza – tomato, mozzarella and black truffles topped with a cracked egg; or Isabella – mozzarella, parma ham and rucola (rocket).

## Spring Court

52-56 Upper Cross Street; tel: 6449 5030; www.springcourt.com.sg; daily 11am–3pm, 6–10.30pm; $$

Established in 1929, this successful family-run restaurant in Chinatown is considered one of the oldest Cantonese restaurants in Singapore. Classics include crisp roast chicken, *popiah* (spring rolls) and golden cereal prawns. Dim sum is available for lunch.

## Thanying

2/F, Amara Hotel, 165 Tanjong Pagar Road; tel: 6222 4688; daily 11am–3pm, 6.30–11pm; $$

This established restaurant serves authentic royal Thai cuisine. The green curry is excellent, as are the stuffed chicken wings and the fragrant olive rice with minced chicken. Be sure to leave room for the delicious dessert buffet.

## Orchard Road

### Basilico

2/F, Regent Hotel, 1 Cuscaden Road; tel:

*Mooncakes*

*It's easy to find tofu-based dishes for vegetarians*

6725 3232; www.regenthotels.com; daily 6.30–10.30am, noon–2.30pm, 6.30–10pm, with exceptions; $$$$

This restaurant by the pool offers alfresco and indoor dining. Aside from the à la carte menu, the outstanding antipasti buffet offers fresh seafood, salads, prosciutto ham with melon, and other Italian-inspired creations. The dessert selection, including Italian cakes, tarts and gelatos, is heavenly.

## Chatterbox

Level 5 Mandarin Orchard, 333 Orchard Road; tel: 6831 6288; www.meritushotels.com/mandarin-orchard-singapore; daily 7–10am, 11am–11pm, until 2am Fri–Sat; $$

The iconic coffee house is most famous for its succulent chicken rice – it is expensive, but worth a try. The other local specialties such as *nasi lemak* (coconut rice with sambal and other condiments) and lobster *laksa* are great for those who like spicy dishes.

## Crystal Jade Palace

04-19 Ngee Ann City, 391 Orchard Road; tel: 6735 2388; www.crystaljade.com; Mon–Sat 11.30am–3pm, 6–10.30pm, Sat 11am–10.30pm, Sun10.30am–11pm; $$

Crystal Jade is famous for its consistently good food. Feast on excellent roast meat and 'live' seafood such as the delicious baked prawns. There is another outlet in the Paragon shopping centre.

## Din Tai Fung

290 Orchard Road, B1-03/06 Paragon; tel:

6836 8336; www.dintaifung.com.sg; Mon–Fri 11am–9.30pm, Sat–Sun 10am–9.30pm; $$

This popular restaurant is always crowded during meal times so queuing may be necessary. Feast on the famous *xiao long bao*, or steamed pork dumplings, and other delicious dishes such as the prawn wonton with chilli oil and wholesome chicken soup.

## Imperial Treasure Nan Bei Restaurant

05-12/13/14 Ngee Ann City, 391 Orchard Road; tel: 6836 6909; www.imperialtreasure.com; Mon–Sat 11.30am–3, 6–11pm, Sun 10.30am–3, 6 –11pm; $$

The Imperial Treasure restaurant empire is known for its consistently good food and prompt service. This outlet boasts top-grade Cantonese dishes, from roast goose to the comforting double-boiled chicken soup.

## Les Amis

02-16 Shaw Centre, 1 Scotts Road; tel: 6733 2225; www.lesamis.com.sg; Mon–Sat noon–2pm, 7–9pm with exceptions; $$$$

This sophisticated restaurant draws well-heeled diners with its exquisite French cuisine, which is light and contemporary with a focus on natural flavours. The award-winning wine list of some 2,000 labels is outstanding. The chic main dining room is illuminated by three antique Parisian chandeliers.

## The Line

22 Orange Grove Road; Lower Lobby, Tower

*Newton Food Centre*

Wing, Shangri-La Hotel; tel: 6213 4398; www. shangri-la.com; daily 6am–midnight; $$$$

The Line exudes loud, exuberant New York chic, thanks to the masterly touches of renowned interior designer Adam D. Tihany. Sixteen culinary stations serve a wide range of international cuisines – from aromatic tandoori chicken to fresh sashimi, all manner of seafood and a lovely dessert spread.

### mezza9

10–12 Scotts Road, Grand Hyatt; tel: 6732 1234; https://singapore.grand.hyatt.com; daily noon–10.30pm; $$$$

This well-known restaurant features show kitchens for sushi, *yakitori*, seafood, Western and Chinese dishes as well as deli and dessert counters, walk-in wine cellar and a Martini bar. You can order from the various show kitchens and watch the chefs in action.

### Newton Food Cente

Bukit Timah Rd (near Newton MRT); daily lunch until late; $

Best visited at night. Ignore the touts, make sure you choose somewhere where prices are posted prominently, and you've got one of Singapore's best local food experiences. Good bets include barbecued seafood, grilled chicken wings, fishball noodles and fried carrot cake.

### The Rice Table

02-09 International Building, 360 Orchard Road; tel: 6835 3782; www.ricetable.com.sg; Mon–Sat noon–3.00pm, 6–10pm; $

Diners love this place for its reasonably priced and substantial *rijstaffel* (rice table) buffet brought straight to the table. Indonesian dishes such as *tahu telor* (tofu omelette), beef *rendang* (spicy beef stew) and satay are firm favourites.

### StraitsKitchen

Grand Hyatt Singapore, 10 Scotts Road; tel: 6732 1234; www.singapore.grand. hyattrestaurants.com/straitskitchen/; Mon–Fri noon–2.30pm, Sat–Sun 12.30–3pm, daily 6–10.30pm; $$$$

Local favourites are served buffet-style at this upscale restaurant. Take your pick from the Indian, Chinese and Malay theatre-kitchens where you can watch chefs whip up your dishes. Highly recommended are the grilled *char kway teow* (fried rice noodles) and tandoori chicken.

## Botanic Gardens and Tanglin Village

### PS Café

28B Harding Road; tel: 9070 8782; www. pscafe.sg; Fri–Sat 8am–midnight, Sun–Thu 8am–11pm; $$$

PS Café is a popular meeting place for the fashionable crowd. Lighter fare like salads and fish and chips are served at lunchtime, and more hearty offerings, such as beef pie and chicken parmigiana, are dished up for dinner.

### The White Rabbit

39C Harding Road; tel: 6473 9965; www. thewhiterabbit.com.sg; Tue–Fri noon–2.30pm, Sat–Sun 10.30am–3pm, Tue–Sun 6.30–

*Fresh seafood at The Line*

10.30pm; $$$$

This charming restaurant-bar is housed in a beautifully restored chapel. Tuck into classic European comfort food such as king crab tagliatelle or macaroni and cheese with truffle sauce and black truffle shavings, followed by a chocolate tart.

## Little India

### Muthu's Curry

138 Race Course Road; tel: 6392 1722; www.muthuscurry.com; daily 10.30am–10.30pm; $$

This restaurant serves a potent fish-head curry – its award-winning speciality – as well as South Indian dishes such as masala chicken and mutton chops cooked in tomato puree and spices – all served on banana leaves.

## Bukit Timah

### Violet's Oon

881 Bukit Timah Road; tel: 9834 9935; https://violetoon.com; Tue–Sun noon–10.30pm; $$

Violet Oon, Singapore's culinary doyenne, runs this casual chic eatery with her son and daughter. Expect to feast on Violet's signature dishes such as *laksa*, chicken curry and a range of Nonya favourites.

## East Coast

### Guan Hoe Soon

38/40 Joo Chiat Place; tel: 6344 2761; www.guanhoesoon.com; daily 10am–3pm, 6–9.30pm; $$

Singapore's oldest Peranakan restaurant was a mere coffee shop when it was founded in 1953 by an enterprising Hain-anese man. You can't go wrong with traditional Straits Chinese dishes such as *satay babi* (pork *satay* curry), *ngo hiang* sausage and *ayam tempra* (chicken stew).

### Jumbo Seafood

01-07/08, 1206 East Coast Parkway; tel: 6442 3435; www.jumboseafood.com.sg; Mon–Fri 5pm–11.45pm, Sat–Sun 11.30am–midnight; $$$

Book in advance if you want to get a table. Outstanding dishes are the chilli crabs, pepper crabs and prawns sautéed with oat cereal, curry leaves and chilli. Ask for an alfresco table facing the sea.

### East Coast Lagoon Food Village

1220 East Coast Parkway, next to car park E2; daily lunch until late; $

Enjoy some of the best local food within a stone's throw of the sea. Make a beeline for the barbecue chicken wings and vermicelli with *satay* sauce. Best visited at night when all the stalls are open.

## Sentosa

### Osia Steak and Seafood Grill restaurant

Resorts World Sentosa, 02-140/141 26 Sentosa Gateway; tel: 6577 6560; www.osiarestaurant.com; Thu–Tue noon–2.30pm, 6–10.30pm; $$$$

Australian celebrity chef Scott Webster has created a menu inspired by fresh Aussie produce and Asian influences. Osia's signature dishes include the black truffle risotto, butter poached lobster and Valrhona hot chocolate soup.

# NIGHTLIFE

Once dismissed as a sterile city with no soul, Singapore has undergone a remarkable transformation into a lively arts and entertainment hub. Whether it's a night of pub-crawling you're after or one of non-stop clubbing, the options are plentiful. There are chill-out alfresco bars set in lush gardens or on rooftops, chic lounges for the design-conscious, pubs with world-class bands, and dance clubs that rank among some of the best in the world.

Better known in international clubbing circles is Zouk, which plays a diet of edgy underground and house music, and has hosted DJ luminaries in the past. In 2016, after 25 years at Jiak Kim Street, Zouk moved into a brand new home within Clarke Quay's Cannery Block. The annual ZoukOut, which began in 2000, is now touted as Asia's largest outdoor dance-music festival. This beach dance party held in December at Sentosa's Siloso Beach lures in throngs of clubbing fans.

Boat Quay might be considered just for tourists, but a fair amount of locals can be seen stumbling out of the bars here too. Many bankers from the CBD area throng these hotspots after work. Further along the river is Clarke Quay, which tempts tourists to its restaurants, bars and dance clubs. Among the home-grown favourites at Clarke Quay is Attica, where DJs spin everything from hip-hop to electronic dance.

Sentosa offers beachside party options, alongside cocktails and bites in a chill-out beach-bar setting. The opening of the integrated resorts in 2010 has also added many vibrant nightlife options including Cé La Vie, perched on the magnificent Sands SkyPark. Marquee Singapore, an immersive nightclub experience with cutting-edge sound across three floors, is poised to join the mix in 2019.

## Civic District

### Loof
331 North Bridge Road; 03-07 Odeon Towers Extension Rooftop; tel: 6337 9416; www.loof.com.sg; Mon–Thu 5pm–1am, Fri–Sat until 2am
This breezy alfresco rooftop bar offers some of the cheapest happy hour drinks in town. Pair refreshing Southeast Asian-inspired cocktails with the delicious local bar bites.

### Bar Rouge
Level 71, Swissôtel The Stamford, 2 Stamford Road; tel: 9177 7307; www.equinoxcomplex.com; Mon–Sun 5pm till late
An intimate clubbing space with a huge selection of cocktails and wines,

*Boat Quay is a major nightlife hub*

located 71 floors up with the most spectacular uninterrupted views of the city. Themed nights, performances and action by the region's hottest DJs.

## Marina Bay

### Cé la vie

SkyPark at Marina Bay Sands Hotel Tower 3, 1 Bayfront Avenue; tel: 6508 2188; http://sg.celavi.com; SkyBar daily noon till late, Club Lounge Mon–Fri noon–10pm, Sat–Sun 11am–10pm, Night Club daily 10am until late, Restaurant daily noon–3pm and 6–11pm

The stunning rooftop setting with the best views in town is a must-visit, whether you're after dining, drinks or just entertainment. Dress code is stylish chic.

### Lantern

80 Collyer Quay, The Fullerton Bay Hotel; tel: 6597 5299; www.fullertonhotel.com; Sun–Thu 10am–1am, Fri–Sat until 2am

Lantern is an outdoor rooftop bar with great views of the marina and beyond. Sink into one of the curvaceous lounge chairs to sip champagne and indulge in gourmet snacks while house music plays in the background. The resident DJ takes to the decks in the evening.

### Post Bar

The Fullerton Hotel, 1 Fullerton Square; tel: 6877 8135; www.fullertonhotel.com; Mon–Wed 3pm–midnight, Thu–Sat until 1am

This trendy bar serves a fine selection of martinis and signature cocktails. The ceiling and pillars of the former General Post Office have been incorporated into a sophisticated and modern interior. Happy hour deals run Mon–Fri 5–8pm and Sat 5pm–midnight. The first Saturday each month is Latino Night, featuring a live band (and cover charge).

## Singapore River

### Attica

01-03 Clarke Quay, 3A River Valley Road; tel: 6333 9973; www.attica.com.sg; Wed–Sat 10pm till late

Attica is a Singapore institution spread across two levels, the first playing R&B and classic hits and

*Post Bar*

*A barman at work*

Level 2 dedicated to house, trance and electro. The two are linked by a courtyard with a lush Balinese garden setting. The club has benefitted from a recent renovation.

### Highlander Bar

01-11 Clarke Quay, 3B River Valley Road; tel: 6235 9528; www.highlanderasia.com; Sun–Mon 6pm–3am, Tue–Fri 5pm–3am, Sat and last two Fri of month 5pm–4am

This Scottish bar demonstrates its theme with wood panelling, antler chandeliers and staff dressed in kilts. Its whisky selection still spans an impressive 250 names, but the bar has geared its emphasis more towards music over the past few years – now with two live band performances and a DJ every night.

### Molly Malone's Irish Pub

56 Circular Road; tel: 6536 2029; www.molly-malone.com; Mon–Wed 11am–1am, Thu until 2am, Fri until 3am, Sat noon–2am

A traditional bar (built in Ireland and transported piece by piece to Singapore) that oozes quaint cosy charm, Molly Malone's is always busy with those with a taste for Irish-style dark beers.

### The Penny Black

26/27 Boat Quay; tel: 6538 2300; https://www.facebook.com/Penny.Black.SG/; Mon–Thu 11.30am–1am, Fri –Sat until 2am, Sun until midnight

Popular with the financial district crowd, this pub serves great lunches – from massaman fish head curry to baked mince beef spaghetti – all washed down with English ales like Ruddles and Old Speckled Hen.

### Zouk

The Cannery, 3C River Valley Road; tel: 6738 2988; www.zoukclub.com; Zouk Wed & Fri–Sat 10pm–4am, Phuture Wed & Fri 10pm–3am, Thu 10pm–2am, Sat & last two Fri of month 10am–4am, Red Tail Bar by Zouk Sun–Tue & Thu 6–11pm, Wed & Fri 7pm–3am, Sat 7pm–4am, Capital 10pm–2am, Fri 10am–3am, Sat & last two Fri of month 10am–4am

One of Singapore's iconic clubs and a world-class venue (named number 3 in *DJ Mag*'s Top 100 Club poll in 2018), Zouk moved into a new home in Clarke Quay in 2016. The club still specialises in electronic dance music, hosting regular appearances by celebrity DJs that have included Hardwell, Tiesto and Disclosure. Phuture's music focus is urban, R&B and hip hop; Capital boasts an island bar, whisky bar, whisky room and seating area; while Red Tail Bar by Zouk serves alluring craft cocktails and sharing bites.

## Orchard Road

### Alley Bar

Peranakan Place, 180 Orchard Road; tel: 6738 8818; www.peranakanplace.com; Sun–Thu 5pm–2am, Fri–Sat until 3am

*Spinning the decks*                    *Live music crowds*

A back alley was transformed into this hip hangout, which draws yuppies to its black terrazzo bar for cocktails such as mojitos and margaritas. Happy hour is from 5–9pm.

### Brotzeit

313 Orchard Road, 01-27, Discovery Walk at 313@Somerset; tel: 6834 4038; http://brotzeit.co; Mon–Thu 11.30am–midnight, Fri 11.30am–1am, Sat 10am–1am, Sun 10am–midnight

Brotzeit (German for 'bread time') gets crowded in the evenings, when expats and executives in the area come here for German beers and Bavarian bites.

### Ice Cold Beer

9 Emerald Hill; tel: 6735 9929; www.ice-cold-beer.com; Sun–Thu 5pm–2am, Fri–Sat until 3am

Occupying a shophouse built in 1910, this bar has ice tanks to ensure that its 60 types of beers are chilled to the right temperature in under 10 minutes. Its 9-inch hotdogs are incredibly good. The resident DJ plays classic rock tunes.

### Martini Bar

10 Scotts Road, Grand Hyatt Singapore; tel: 6738 1234; Mon–Thu 5pm–midnight, Fri–Sat 5pm–1am, Sun 3pm–midnight

This incredibly popular bar adjacent to Mezza9 restaurant is famous for its variety of special martini concoctions (there are over 30 hand-crafted martinis in the menu). Bar bites such as crab cakes are made using high-quality ingredients.

### Muddy Murphy's Irish Pub

442 Orchard Road; tel: 6735 0400; Sun–Thu 11am–1am, Fri–Sat until 2am

One of the earliest Irish pubs to open in Singapore, Muddy Murphy's continues to thrive. In 1996, the bar was designed and built to scale in Dublin, then disassembled, shipped to Singapore and reassembled. Enjoy live music and live televised sports alongside pub grub, Guinness and Kilkenny ale.

## Sentosa

### Tanjong Beach Club

120 Tanjong Beach Walk; tel: 6270 1355; www.tanjongbeachclub.com; Tue–Fri 11am–10pm, Sat 10am–1pm, Sun 9am–10pm

A great place to unwind by the beach. Check out the string of parties held here throughout the year. Special cocktails feature local ingredients.

### Wavehouse Sentosa

36 Siloso Beach Walk; tel: 6377 3113; www.wavehousesentosa.com; Mon–Fri 11.30am–9.30pm, Sat–Sun 10.30am–10.30pm

A simulated surfing, dining and lifestyle venue where partygoers can enjoy live music and late night parties at the beach bar. Enjoy music by top DJs, as well as local and international acts.

*Children on a trip to Singapore Zoo*

# A–Z

## A

### Addresses

For high-rise apartments or buildings, addresses begin with the block or building number, then the street name and unit number followed by the postal code, e.g. Block 56, Bedok North Street 3, #03-04, Singapore 469623. For landed properties, the address is written as 52 Napier Road, Singapore 258500.

## B

### Budgeting

Singapore has the second-highest standard of living in Asia (behind Japan), so expect many prices to be only slightly below those in North America and northern Europe. Flights from London to Singapore cost about £800, from the US about US$1700, and from Australia about AU$800. Food and transportation can be bargains. Meals at hawker centres and food courts can be as little as S$3. A three-course dinner in a mid-range restaurant can cost about S$50–70. Subway (MRT) and bus cash fares are between S$1.40 and S$2.50, and taxi trips around town are often as little as S$10. Hotels run the gamut, from under S$70 per room for budget

choices to about S$150 for a mid-range double room, to over S$500 for top accommodation. Private city tours are priced at S$28–100 and up.

Entrance fees to sights are reasonable (S$2–18), but entertainment costs (for performances, nightclubs) can be as high as in Western capitals. Alcohol is expensive, around S$10 for a pint of beer and $12 for a glass of house wine. Many bars have a 'happy hour', usually between 5pm and 9pm, with deals such as half-price drinks.

Budget travellers can certainly visit Singapore cheaply, although other nearby Southeast Asian destinations offer much lower prices. Singapore offers convenience, cleanliness, efficiency, superb meals and some great attractions, but it is not the bargain basement of Asia.

### Business hours

Museums and tourist attractions have varying hours, but many open at about 9.30am and close at 5 or 6pm; some are closed at least one day a week. Banks are usually open Monday to Friday 9.30am–3pm, Saturdays 9.30am–12.30pm (but Saturday hours can vary). Government offices operate Monday to Friday 8am–6pm; some are open on Saturday. Many restaurants are open daily 11.30am–10pm, but hawker centres

*A traditional shophouse*

keep longer hours, from dawn to midnight daily. Department stores and shopping centres are generally open daily from 10am–9pm.

## Children

Singapore is a safe place with plenty of family-friendly places. Some places in Singapore have attained the 'Pro-family Business' accreditation, such as Singapore Zoo, Night Safari and several family-friendly malls. Children are usually given concessions on entrance fees.

## Climate

As Singapore is located 137km (85 miles) north of the equator, the weather usually varies between hot and very hot. Temperatures range between 33°C (91°F) and 24°C (75°F), with high humidity levels from 64 to 98 percent. Most of the rain falls during the northeast monsoon between November and February and to a lesser degree during the southwest monsoon from May to September. Thunderstorms can occur throughout the year.

## Clothing

Bring along light cotton wear and comfortable shoes for walking. Sandals and sunglasses are useful. Umbrellas and raincoats are always handy as downpours are unpredictable.

If you are planning a night out in town, bring along something dressier alongside proper shoes (not sandals or sportswear). You are welcome to step into the mosques and Hindu temples but before entering, remove your footwear. Note that mosques require that arms and legs be fully covered (by long-sleeved shirts, long trousers and long skirts or sarongs) to enter. Sikh temples require visitors to wear a head covering, as do synagogues for males.

Smart-casual attire will see you through most occasions in Singapore, where normal office attire is a shirt and tie for men, with jackets reserved for more formal occasions. Dress to cope with the heat when outdoors and have a wrap or light cardigan for the sharp drop in temperature inside some air-conditioned buildings. Shorts and T-shirts are acceptable in many places, although many clubs and some restaurants have stricter dress codes.

## Crime and safety

Singapore has one of the lowest crime rates in the world. Although it is generally a safe place, beware of pickpockets, especially in crowded areas. Place valuables in your hotel safe before heading out. It is generally safe for women to walk around alone, even at night.

Singapore has strict laws covering infractions that might be considered

*Visiting Sri Veeramakaliamman Temple*

minor elsewhere. Littering can result in a S$300 fine for first-time offenders. Smoking is banned in public places, including restaurants, buses and taxis; the fine is up to S$1,000. The chewing of gum is not banned, but the unauthorised sale of chewing gum is subject to a fine up to S$2,000.

Drug offences are dealt with harshly. The death penalty is mandatory for those convicted of trafficking, manufacturing, importing or exporting certain amounts of drugs.

## Customs

Visitors carrying more than the equivalent of S$30,000 in cash or cheque have to declare this fact to the customs authorities upon arrival. Duty-free allowance per adult is 1 litre of spirits, 1 litre of wine or port and 1 litre of beer, stout or ale. No duty-free cigarettes are allowed into Singapore although they may be purchased on the way out. Duty-free purchases can be made both upon arrival and departure except when returning to Singapore within 48 hours. This is to prevent Singaporeans from making a day trip out of the country to stock up on duty-free goods. Passengers arriving from Malaysia are not allowed duty-free concessions.

The list of prohibited items includes drugs (the penalty for even small amounts can be death), firecrackers, obscene or seditious materials, endangered wildlife or their by-prod-

ucts, reproduction of copyright publications, video tapes, video compact discs, laser discs, records or cassettes, chewing tobacco and imitation tobacco products, cigarette lighters of pistol or revolver shape, and chewing gum (except dental or nicotine gum). For more information, contact **Immigration & Checkpoints Authority** (www.ica.gov.sg) and **Singapore Customs** (www.customs.gov.sg).

## Disabled travellers

There is a growing awareness of the special needs of disabled people. The **National Council of Social Service** (tel: 6210 2500; www.ncss.org.sg) is a good information source. The **Disabled People's Association Singapore** (tel: 6791 1134; www.dpa.org.sg) is another; http://www.dpa.org.sg/resources/accessible-singapore-for-tourists/ is particularly useful for visitors. Some of the newer buildings are designed with the disabled in mind but generally, getting around by public transport for the wheelchair-bound is a problem. There are some taxis that are large enough to accommodate wheelchairs but these have to be booked ahead.

## Electricity

Electrical supply is on a 220–240 volt, 50 Hz system. Most hotels have

*Chinese temples are less formal than other religious houses*

transformers for 110–120 volt, 60 Hz appliances.

## Embassies

**Australia:** 25 Napier Road, tel: 6836 4100; www.singapore.embassy.gov.au
**Britain:** 100 Tanglin Road, tel: 6424 4200; www.ukinsingapore.fco.gov.uk
**Canada:** 11-01 One George Street, tel: 6854 5900; www.singapore.gc.ca
**New Zealand:** 21-04, One George Street, tel: 6235 9966; www.nzembassy.com/singapore
**USA:** 27 Napier Road, tel: 6476 9100; https://sg.usembassy.gov

## Emergencies

**Fire and ambulance:** 995
**Police:** 999 (emergency), 1800-255 0000 (non-emergency)
**STB Tourist Information Hotline:** 1800-736 2000

## Etiquette

Most good behaviour in Singapore is law-enforced; public signage is usually very good and there are clear signs explaining what to do and what not to do.

**Road crossing:** Pedestrians must use a designated crossing if one is available within 50 metres (165ft), or else risk a fine of up to S$1,000 for jaywalking. Designated crossings are zebra crossings, overhead bridges, underpasses, and traffic-light junctions fitted with red and green pedestrian signal lights.

**Littering:** The government has taken great pains, not only to keep Singapore's streets clean, but also to inculcate civic-conscious habits in its citizens. Litter bins are found everywhere and make it inexcusable to litter. First-time offenders are fined S$300 (be it a bus ticket, a cigarette butt or a sweet wrapper). Repeat offenders are also sentenced to participate in a corrective work order programme, where they have to collect rubbish in a public place for a period of time, or pay up to S$5,000 in fines.

**Toilets:** Failure to flush urinals and water closets after use in public toilets (hotels, shopping complexes, etc) can result in a S$150 fine. It is interesting to note, however, that to date no one has ever been convicted of this offence. Still, take no chances.

**Chewing gum:** Contrary to belief, you won't go to jail for chewing gum. The ban – imposed in 1992 because the authorities got fed up with people sticking wads of used gum on train and cinema seats – covers only the sale and importation of chewing gum, not the actual act of gum-chewing. Remember only to chew the gum, not hawk it at street corners or stick it under seats when no one is looking. Note: A new law passed in 2003 allows the sale of gum with therapeutic value, for instance, nicotine-laced gum to help smokers kick the habit. These items can only be bought from the pharmacist, not off the shelves.

**Public transport**: No eating, drinking or smoking is allowed aboard buses and MRT trains. And passengers are banned from carrying smelly durians on board MRT trains too!

**Religious and cultural habits**: When keeping company with Muslims and Hindus, you should be careful neither to eat nor offer anything with your left hand. Removing one's shoes before entering a mosque or an Indian temple has been a tradition for centuries. Inside, devotees do not smoke, yet neither of these customs generally apply to Chinese temples, where more informal styles prevail. Visitors are most welcome to look around at their leisure and stay for religious rituals, except in some mosques. While people pray, it is understood that those not participating in the service will stand aside. A polite gesture would be to ask permission before taking photographs: the request is seldom, if ever, refused. Modest clothing is appropriate for a visit. Most temples and mosques have a donation box for funds to help maintain the building. It is customary for visitors to contribute a token amount before leaving.

**F**

## Festivals

Although the dates of ethnic festivals vary because they are based on the lunar calendar, most are confined to one or two specific months of the year. The only exception is the Muslim festival of Hari Raya Puasa, which advances by a month or so each year. The other major Muslim festival is Hari Raya Haji, which marks the sacrifices made by Muslims who make the pilgrimage to Mecca.

### January/February

**Lunar New Year** is the most important festival for the Chinese. A colourful parade called **Chingay** is held, with cultures from all over the world celebrated. Also during this period is the Indian harvest festival of **Pongal**. Then comes the Indian festival of **Thaipusam** where devotees go into a trance and perform acts of penance.

### March/April

**Good Friday**, which precedes Easter, is observed at many Christian churches in Singapore. Also around this time the Chinese observe **Qing Ming** in remembrance of deceased ancestors and loved ones.

The **World Gourmet Summit** and **Singapore Film Festival** are also held during these months.

### May/June/July

**Vesak Day** (May) commemorates Buddha's birth, enlightenment and death. The **Dragon Boat Festival** (June) is held in remembrance of the poet Qu Yuan, who drowned himself in protest against political corruption in China. The annual **Singapore Arts**

**Festival** (May/June) brings top-rate performers from around the world. The **Great Singapore Sale** (end of May to mid-July) is an island-wide shopping extravaganza. The **Singapore Food Festival** is held in July.

### August/September

To celebrate **National Day** on 9 August, a parade and mass displays are held at the Marina Bay Floating Stadium; the evening ends with a fireworks display. The **Mooncake Festival** coincides with what is believed to be the year's brightest full moon during the eighth lunar month.

### October/November/December

The most important Hindu festival **Deepavali** is in October/November. **ZoukOut**, an annual dance party is held at Sentosa's Siloso Beach. Orchard Road lights up for **Christmas**, and the year winds up with carols being sung in the streets and parties.

# H

## Health

Singapore has no free medical care, so be sure you are covered by insurance. Most hotels have doctors on call. The local water from the tap is treated and safe for drinking. Strict control is exercised over the hygiene of food sold, from hawker stalls to hotels. If you require treatment, there are more than 20 government and private hospitals as well as umpteen number of clinics for any eventuality. Singapore's medical facilities are the finest in Asia; the number of foreigners seeking treatment here is high. Consultation fees start from about S\$30 in a private practice.

### Hospitals

**Mount Elizabeth Hospital:** 3 Mount Elizabeth; tel: 6737 2666; www.mountelizabeth.com.sg
**Raffles Hospital:** 585 North Bridge Road; tel: 6311 1111; www.rafflesmedicalgroup.com
**Singapore General Hospital:** Outram Road; tel: 6222 3322; www.sgh.com.sg

### Pharmacies

These are open 9am–6pm, sometimes later, but it is wise to travel with your own prescriptions and medications.

# I

## Internet

**Wireless@SG** is a scheme that provides free wireless connection at selected hotspots. You will need to register online with a service provider: M1 (tel: 6655 5633; www.m1net.com.sg/Wireless-SG), Starhub (tel: 6873 2828; www.starhub.com/wsg), **Singtel** (tel: 1688; www.singtel.com/wirelessSG) or Y5ZONE (tel: 6491 9652;

*Getting inspiration at a photography exhibit*

www.y5zone.sg). See https://www.imda.gov.sg/wireless-sg for more information.

# L

## Left luggage

Bags can be stored at the Changi Airport's Left Baggage counters at Terminal 1 (tel: 6214 0318), Terminal 2 (tel: 6214 1683) and Terminal 3 (tel: 6242 8936). There is also a place to store luggage at Terminal 4 (no telephone; Level 1, Public Area; Level 2M, Departure Hall, Transit Hall). Alternatively, check with any of the airport's information desks.

## LGBTQ travellers

Engaging in homosexual activity is an offence, but it does not mean it is non-existent. In fact, several establishments now attract an LGBTQ crowd. In general Singapore society is still fairly conservative when it comes to public displays of gay affection, and these actions are likely to draw stares. But that is about as much a reaction as you will get as Singaporeans do not usually react aggressively to homosexuality.

The local gay rights advocacy group **PLU3** has not been allowed to register as a legitimate society, but some useful websites on Signapore's LGBTQ scene can be found at www.fridae.asia/agenda/singapore and www.utopia-asia.com.

## Lost property

The loss of your passport or valuables should be reported immediately to the police. To lodge a police report, visit the nearest police station or call 1800-255 0000. For lost items in taxies, on buses and MRT trains, contact the respective transport service operator.

# M

## Media

Of the nine major daily newspapers published in Singapore, four are in English, led by *The Straits Times*, which covers local, regional and international news. *The Edge Singapore* is a business and investment weekly. Local magazines in English include *S–G*, *Time Out*, *Where Singapore* and *8 Days*, all of which cover entertainment, attractions and shopping. International newspapers and magazines are available at bookstores, newsstands, shopping centres and hotel kiosks. Some publications are subject to government-controlled circulation quotas.

Cable and satellite TV broadcasts, with CNN, BBC, MTV, NHK, ESPN and other common channels, are widely available in hotels. Local TV stations broadcast via the following channels: Channel 5 in English, Channel 8 and Channel U in Mandarin, Suria in Malay, Vasantham in Tamil. Okto

*It's easy to find newspapers and magazines*

shows kids' programmes, documentaries and arts content and Channel NewsAsia broadcasts news and current affairs programmes.

Eight of the local radio stations broadcast in English. Popular stations for English music include Class 95 (95FM), Gold 90FM (90.5FM) and 987FM (98.7FM). BBC World Service is also available on FM radio (88.9FM).

## Money

**Currency.** The Singapore dollar (abbreviated S$ or SGD) is divided into 100 cents, with coins of 1, 5, 10, 20, 50 cents and S$1. Bills in common circulation are S$2, S$5, S$10, S$20, S$50, S$100, S$500, S$1,000 and S$10,000.

**Currency exchange.** Money-changing services are available at Changi Airport and at most banks, hotels and shopping centres. Licensed money changers (usually located in shopping malls) give slightly better rates than banks; hotels give the worst rates. The exchange rates at the airport are on a par with those at downtown banks.

**Credit cards.** Major credit cards are widely accepted by Singapore's restaurants, hotels, shops, travel agencies and taxis. Report lost or stolen credit cards to the police (tel: 1800-353 0000). In Singapore, you can call American Express (tel: 1800-299-1997), Diners Club (tel: 6416 0800), Mastercard (tel: 800-110 0113) and

Visa (tel: 800-448 1250) for replacements.

**ATMs.** Automated teller machines are everywhere (at banks, shopping malls and many hotels). The Cirrus and plus system machines work in Singapore just as they do overseas.

# P

## Postal services

Postal services are fast and efficient. Most hotels will handle mail for you or you may post letters and parcels at any post office. The **Singapore Post** branch at 1 Killiney Road is open Mon–Fri 9am–9pm, Sat 9.30am–4pm, and Sun and public 10.30am–4pm; the branch at the Changi Airport's Terminal 2 is open Mon–Fri 9am–6pm. Call 6734 7899, or 1605; or check www.singpost.com for more information about postal rates, express mail and other services, including its courier service called SpeedPost. Post boxes are white in colour with a Singapore post logo. DHL, FedEx, TNT and UPS provide courier services as well.

## Public holidays

**New Year's Day:** 1 January
**Chinese New Year:** January/February
**Good Friday:** April
**Labour Day:** 1 May
**Vesak Day:** May
**National Day:** 9 August
**Deepavali:** October/November

**Christmas Day:** 25 December
**Hari Raya Puasa:** date varies
**Hari Raya Haji:** date varies

# R

## Religion

Buddhism and Taoism are most commonly practised by the Chinese, among whom about 20 percent are Christians. Malays are predominantly Muslim and Singaporeans of Indian descent are mainly Hindu, Sikh or Christian. The Eurasians and Peranakans are largely Christians, either Roman Catholic or Protestant.

# T

## Telephones

The country code for Singapore is 65. International calls to Singapore are made by dialling the international access code for the originating country, followed by Singapore's country code and the eight-digit local number. International calls from Singapore are made by dialling the international access code (001, 013 or 019) followed by the country code, area code and local number. No area codes are used within Singapore. Dial 100 for local call assistance and 104 for overseas call assistance.

Most telephones in Singapore operate using phone cards (stored value cards), which can be purchased from all post offices and convenience stores like 7 Eleven, and be used for making local and overseas calls. International calling cards can be used from any phone; simply dial the calling card's access number for Singapore and follow the instructions.

**Mobile phones.** Only users of GSM mobile phones with global roaming service can connect automatically with Singapore's phone networks. If you are planning to be in Singapore for any length of time, it is more economical to buy a local SIM card from one of the three service providers: Singtel (tel: 1626 or 6738 0123), M1 (tel: 1627 or 1800-843 8383) or Starhub (tel: 1633 or 6820 1633). These cards give you a local mobile number and cost a minimum of S$20. All local mobile numbers begin with '8' or '9'.

## Tourist information

The **Singapore Tourism Board** (STB) is a superb organisation, offering mountains of free and helpful literature to visitors. Their website is www.visitsingapore.com.

STB offices abroad include the following:

**Australia:** Level 11, AWA Building, 47 York Street, Sydney NSW 2000; tel: 02-9290 2888 or 9290 2882; email: stb_infosingapore@stb.gov.sg

**UK:** Singapore Centre, First floor, Southwest House, 11A Regent Street, London SW1Y 4LR; tel: 020-7484 2710; email: stb_london@stb.gov.sg

*Ornate Chinese temple detail*

**US:** 1156 Avenue of the Americas, Suite 702, New York, NY 10036; tel: 212-302 4861; email: newyork@stb.gov.sg

The Singapore Tourism Board runs a 24-hour tourist information hotline: 1800-736 2000 (toll-free in Singapore), 65-6736 2000 (from overseas); 1 Orchard Spring Lane, Tourism Court; Mon–Fri 9am–6pm. Visitor centres are at the following locations:

**Singapore Visitors Centre @ Orchard:** Junction of Cairnhill Road and Orchard Road (daily 8.30am–9.30pm).

**Singapore Visitors Centre @ ION Orchard:** Level 1 Concierge (daily 10am–10pm).

**Chinatown Visitor Centre @ Kreta Ayer Square:** 2 Banda Street, behind Buddha Tooth Relic Temple and Museum (daily 9am–9pm).

## Time zone

Singapore is 8 hours ahead of GMT.

## Transport

### Getting around

**From the airport:** There are several easy ways of getting to town from the airport. Taxis, airport shuttles and city bus No 36 are available at terminal entrances. A taxi ride downtown (a 16km/10-mile journey) costs about S$20–40, excluding surcharges (Fri–Sun 5pm–midnight S$5; S$3 all other times; additional surcharge of 50 percent of final metered fare daily midnight–6am). Limousine taxis cost $55 and seven-seater taxis cost $60. Taxi rides from the airport to downtown take about 20 to 30 minutes. It's also possible to take the MRT link from the airport to Tanah Merah station and to take a westbound train from there to get to the city centre.

**Taxis:** Singapore's 25,000 taxis are air-conditioned and comfortable. Most of the drivers are friendly and helpful, although a few can be a bit gruff. Within the CBD (including Orchard Road) taxis can only be boarded and alighted at taxi stands and alongside roads; elsewhere in Singapore, simply flag one along the road. All taxis are metered; most accept credit cards. Basic fares are S$3–3.40 (normal taxi) or S$3.90 (limousine taxi) for the first kilometre, and 22 cents for every 400 metres travelled up to 10km, or every 350 metres travelled after 10km, and every 45 seconds of waiting time.

A variety of surcharges are thrown in for midnight to 6am trips (50 percent is added to the meter fare), peak period travel, travel into restricted downtown zones, advanced booking and airport travel. Under the ERP (Electronic Road Pricing) system, additional charges apply when the taxi passes ERP gantry points during its hours of operation.

The major taxi companies are Comfort Taxi (tel: 6552 1111), SMRT (tel: 6555 8888), Prime Taxi (tel: 6778 0808), Premier Taxi (tel: 6363 6888), Yellow-Top Taxi (tel: 6293 5545) and TransCab (tel: 6555 3333).

*Shoppers on Orchard Road*

**Cars:** Car hire is seldom necessary in Singapore since it is compact and served by excellent and inexpensive forms of public transportation, but major car rental companies operate all over the island, including at the airport and downtown in the hotel districts. A valid driver's licence from your country of residence or a valid International Driving Licence is required, as is a major credit card.

Motorists drive on the left, overtake on the right and yield to pedestrians at designated crossing points. Speed limits are 50–60 kmh (30–37 mph) in residential areas, 70–90 kmh (40–50 mph) on expressways. Singapore roads are in excellent condition and signposted in English. Speed cameras are installed throughout the island. Bus lanes or lanes with unbroken yellow lines are used only by buses during rush hours (Mon–Fri 7.30–9.30am and 5–8pm). Full-day bus lanes (Mon–Sat 7.30am–8pm) are marked by red lines.

**Buses:** Singapore has an efficient public bus system (www.sbstransit.com.sg or www.smrt.com.sg). Buses operate daily from 6am to midnight. Bus fares are between $1.40 and S$2.50 for air-conditioned buses. Ask the driver for the fare to your destination; exact change is required and the money is deposited into a box near the driver. Be aware, however, that the authorities are aiming to turn the public transport system completely cash-free by 2020. Try to purchase a Singapore Tourist Pass or an ez-link card (see below).

You can purchase the **Singapore Tourist Pass** (tel: 6496 8300; www.thesingaporetouristpass.com.sg) at selected MRT stations. Enjoy unlimited rides on buses and trains for just S$10 a day. Also available are 2-day (S$16) and 3-day (S$20) passes (with a refundable deposit of S$10 per card). To use the card, either flash or tap it on the electronic readers mounted at bus entrances and entry turnstiles of MRT stations.

If you are planning to be in Singapore for a longer period, buy an **ez-link card** (stored-value transportation card). This costs S$12 (out of which S$7 is stored value for use) if purchased from Transit Link Ticket Offices, Concession Card Replacement Centres or Passenger Service Centres. Cards bought from 7-Eleven cost S$10, with S$5 stored value. The remaining S$5 is a non-refundable administration charge, but the convenience of using this card far outweighs the expense. Simply tap the card on the electronic reader as you board and alight the bus. As part of the scheme to turn the public transport system cash-free by 2020, many ticketing machines no longer accept cash, only electronic methods such as debit or credit cards. Make sure you carry plastic and don't get caught out.

**NightRider.** SMRT night buses run from 11.30pm–2am on Friday, Satur-

*Sightseeing tour bus in Little India*

day and evenings of public holidays. Trips cost a flat fee of S$4.50. They provide an inexpensive way of getting around late at night. The routes pass major nightlife areas, including Boat Quay, Clarke Quay, Marina Bay and Orchard Road. Check www.smrt.com.sg for detailed routes.

**Nite Owl.** SBS Transit runs night buses from midnight to 2am on Friday, Saturday and evenings of public holidays. Trips cost a flat fee of S$4.40. Check details at www.sbstransit.com.sg.

**SIA Hop-On** is a tourist bus service that plies the major landmarks and attractions around the city area. As its name implies, you hop on (and off) as you wish along various designated stops. Check www.siahopon.com for more info or call 6338 6877.

**Subway (MRT):** Singapore's Mass Rapid Transit (MRT) system is very efficient and simple to use. It operates from 5.30am to around 1am daily, with trains arriving every 2 to 3 minutes from 7am to 9am and 5 to 7 minutes during off-peak times. Single trip tickets cost between S$1.40 and $2.50, in addition to a S$1 refundable deposit. Because this can prove cumbersome (and in light of the transport system phasing in a cash-free initiative by 2020), it makes more sense to get the Singapore Tourist Pass or an ez-link fare card (see above) even if you're just visiting the country for a day. Rush hours should be avoided. For information, tel: 1800-336 8900, Mon–Fri 7.30am–6.30pm; www.smrt.com.sg. There are five MRT lines: the East–West, North–South, Northeast, Circle and Downtown lines. A sixth line, the Thomson-East Coast Line, is currently under construction and is scheduled to start operating in 2019.

**Trishaws.** Trishaw Uncle (www.trishawuncle.com.sg; tel: 6337 7111) is the only licensed operator for trishaw tours in Singapore appointed by the Singapore Tourism Board. The pick-up point is at the Albert Mall Trishaw Park at Queen Street.

## Visas and passports

Visa requirements can vary, so check with a Singapore embassy or consular office in your home country.

## Websites

www.changiairport.com.sg Changi Airport

www.stayinsingapore.com Online hotel bookings

www.visitsingapore.com Singapore Tourism Board (STB)

www.gov.sg Official Singapore government site

www.makansutra.com Details the best hawker fare

www.hungrygowhere.com Food reviews and listings

www.sistic.com.sg Tickets for performing arts and athletic events

*A scene from 'Ilo Ilo'*

# BOOKS AND FILM

Most of the Singapore's literary works portray and explore various aspects of society. Given the small domestic market, it cannot be said that local literature has a huge following. Yet that doesn't mean that the Singaporeans aren't voracious readers. Major bookshops like Kinokuniya continue to see a healthy crowd. Like their outlook in life, Singaporeans' tastes in books are international.

Over the last few years, the leading non-fiction author has been Singapore's former prime minister Lee Kwan Yew. Considered the founder of modern Singapore, Lee has written two books, which sold out within days of their release. Other well-known books include Goh Poh Seng's *If We Dream Too Long*, widely recognised as the first true Singaporean novel. Catherine Lim is Singapore's most widely read author – largely due to her first two books of short stories, *Little Ironies: Stories of Singapore* and *Or Else, the Lightning God and Other Stories*.

Singaporeans love going to the movies – which explains the glut of cineplexes across the island. They enjoy a good Hollywood blockbuster, so much so that some movies open here even before they do in the US. For the most part, Singaporean films are slowly but steadily winning critical and commercial success, both at home and abroad.

Singapore had its golden age of cinema in the 1950s and 1960s when it was home to two powerhouse movie studios, Cathay and Shaw Brothers. Following Singapore's separation from Malaysia in 1965, the film industry moved to Kuala Lumpur. The 1990s saw a revival for the film industry. Director Eric Khoo's *12 Storeys* (1997) was the first Singaporean film shown at the Cannes Film Festival. But it was local TV comic-turned-filmmaker Jack Neo's *Money No Enough* (1998) that really warmed Singaporeans to local filmmaking efforts. In 2013, *Ilo Ilo* premiered at the Cannes Film Festival as part of the Directors' Fortnight, and the film was the first Singaporean feature film to win the Camera d'Or award.

To celebrate Singapore's 50th anniversary in 2015, five Southeast Asian filmmakers – Apichatpong Weerasethakul (Thailand), Brilliante Mendoza (Philippines), Eric Khoo (Singapore), Ho Yuhang (Malaysia) and Joko Anwar (Indonesia) came together to make an omnibus of short stories collectively entitled *Art Through Our Eyes*.

## Books

**Complete Notes from Singapore: The Omnibus Edition** (Neil Humphreys)
A British humourist writes on Singapore's idiosyncracies.

**Conversations with Lee Kuan Yew** (Tom Plate)
This candid, one-on-one conversation with the internationally respected political

*The critically acclaimed 'My Magic'*

leader is startling and even humorous at times.

**Lee Kuan Yew: Hard Truths to Keep Singapore Going (various)**
This tome compiled by local writers is based on 32 hours of interviews at the Istana with Singapore's influential former Prime Minister.

**The New Mrs Lee's Cookbook Vol. 1 and 2 (Shermay Lee)**
A delightful introduction to Peranakan cuisine and culture plus well thought-out recipes.

**One Fierce Hour (Alfian Sa'at)**
Highly charged poems about life in Singapore by this acclaimed poet and playwright.

**The Shrimp People (Rex Shelley)**
An evocative tale on Singapore's Eurasians that won the National Book Prize.

**Shiok!: Exciting Tropical Asian Flavours (Terry Tan and Christopher Tan)**
One of the best books on Singaporean cuisine, with well-written, and tried-and-tested recipes.

**Singapore: Architecture of a Global City (Robert Powell, Albert K.S. Lim and Li Lian Chee)**
Focuses on the city's modern architecture and skyline.

## Films

**12 Storeys** (1997)
Director Eric Khoo's indulgently lengthy frames capture the lives of lonely residents in a block of flats. The only Singaporean film to date to be selected for the Un Certain Regard section at Cannes.

**15** (2002)
This film, directed by Royston Tan, about restless Chinese teenagers who turn to gangs was heavily censored on release (references to gangs are considered risky in Singapore). It's available uncut only in the UK and US.

**Be With Me** (2005)
Inspired by the life story of Theresa Chan, an elderly woman who has been deaf and blind since she was a teenager, this Eric Khoo film is made up of three poignant stories interwoven around the desire for love and companionship. It was the opening film for the Directors' Fortnight programme at Cannes in 2005.

**My Magic** (2008)
After the screening of My Magic at the 61st Cannes Film Festival, a 15-minute standing ovation ensued. The Eric Khoo film – a mostly Tamil drama about an alcoholic magician struggling to repair his relationship with his young son – was Singapore's first contender for the Palme d'Or.

**Ah Boys To Men** (2012–3)
Jack Neo's successful two-part film revolves around the lives of a group of recruits serving their National Service in Singapore. It is to date the highest-grossing Singaporean movie of all time.

**Pop Aye** (2017)
Directed by Kirsten Tan, this movie tells the story of a disenchanted architect who bumps into his long-lost elephant on the streets of Bangkok. They both embark on a journey across Thailand, in search of the farm where they grew up together.

# ABOUT THIS BOOK

This *Explore Guide* has been produced by the editors of Insight Guides, whose books have set the standard for visual travel guides since 1970. With top-quality photography and authoritative recommendations, these guidebooks bring you the very best routes and itineraries in the world's most exciting destinations.

## BEST ROUTES

The routes in the book provide something to suit all budgets, tastes and trip lengths. As well as covering the destination's many classic attractions, the itineraries track lesser-known sights, and there are also excursions for those who want to extend their visit outside the city. The routes embrace a range of interests, so whether you are an art fan, a gourmet, a history buff or have kids to entertain, you will find an option to suit.

We recommend reading the whole of a route before setting out. This should help you to familiarise yourself with it and enable you to plan where to stop for refreshments – options are shown in the 'Food and Drink' box at the end of each tour.

For our pick of the tours by theme, consult Recommended Routes for... (see pages 6–7).

## INTRODUCTION

The routes are set in context by this introductory section, giving an overview of the destination to set the scene, plus background information on food and drink, shopping and more, while a succinct history timeline highlights the key events over the centuries.

## DIRECTORY

Also supporting the routes is a Directory chapter, with a clearly organised A–Z of practical information, our pick of where to stay while you are there and select restaurant listings; these eateries complement the more low-key cafés and restaurants that feature within the routes and are intended to offer a wider choice for evening dining. Also included here are some nightlife listings and our recommendations for books and films about the destination.

## ABOUT THE AUTHORS

This guide to Singapore was written by Malaysian-born journalist and writer Amy Van. Amy has lived in Singapore for more than 15 years and calls Singapore her home. With more than a decade of editorial experience, she contributes to a variety of food, travel and lifestyle publications in the region as well as international travel guides. She has also worked on numerous book projects for Insight Guides, among others, as writer and editor.

## CONTACT THE EDITORS

We hope you find this Explore Guide useful, interesting and a pleasure to read. If you have any questions or feedback on the text, pictures or maps, please do let us know. If you have noticed any errors or outdated facts, or have suggestions for places to include on the routes, we would be delighted to hear from you. Please drop us an email at hello@insightguides.com. Thanks!

# CREDITS

**Explore Singapore**
**Editor:** Helen Fanthorpe
**Author:** Amy Van, updated by Paul Stafford
**Head of DTP and Pre-Press:** Rebeka Davies
**Picture Editor:** Tom Smyth
**Cartography:** original cartography Berndtson & Berndtson, updated by Carte
**Photo credits:** 123RF 80, 124; Alamy 84, 121 B, 136, 137; Apa Publications 36, 37L, 38, 54, 64, 64/65, 65L, 66, 67, 68, 69, 70, 71, 72, 73, 75, 76, 77, 82, 89, 91, 94, 95L; AWL Images 1; Dreamstime 4ML, 4MC, 8MR, 10/11, 16/17, 18, 30MR, 87L; Fairmont Hotels 104, 105; Fullerton Hotel 102MC; Getty Images 6MC, 28, 53, 56, 97, 99, 100, 100/101; Hyatt 109B; IndoChine Group 112; iStock 7MR, 8/9T, 20, 21, 26, 26/27, 30/31T, 33, 44/45, 46, 47L, 48/49, 52, 57, 58, 58/59, 59L, 60/61, 63L, 78/79, 82/83, 83L, 85, 86, 86/87, 88, 96; Leonardo 46/47, 62, 102/103T, 108, 109; Marina Bay Sands 27L, 30ML, 102MR, 106/107, 112/113, 113L, 114, 114/115, 115L; Marina Mandarin 102MC; National Museum of Singapore 41; Nikt Wong/Apa Publications 90, 93, 94/95, 98, 130; Peranakan Museum 40; Photoshot 29; Raffles Hotel 30ML, 102MR, 102ML; Rasa Sentosa 102ML;Shangri-La Hotel 8MC, 110/111, 119; Shutterstock 118; Singapore Art Museum 43; Singapore Tourism Board 4MC, 4ML, 6ML, 7T, 7MR, 8MR, 8ML, 10, 11L, 16, 17L, 19, 22, 23, 24/25, 25L, 32, 36/37, 42, 55, 62/63, 81, 92, 116, 116/117, 122, 122/123, 123L, 125, 126; Singapore Tourism Board/Charles Loh 34; STB/Christopher White 128/129; STB/Joseph Goh Meng Huat 8ML; Swissotel Hotels & Resorts 4MR; The Arts House 35; Timothy Hursley/Marina Bay Sands 6TL; Vincent Ng/Apa Publications 4MR, 4/5T, 6BC, 7M, 8MC, 12, 13, 14, 15, 24, 30MC, 30MC, 30MR, 39, 50, 51, 74, 117L, 120/121, 127, 131, 132/133, 134, 135; Wildlife Reserves Singapore 101L
**Cover credits:** Maurizio Rellini/4Corners Images (main) iStock (bottom)

Printed by CTPS – China
All Rights Reserved
© 2019 Apa Digital (CH) AG and Apa Publications (UK) Ltd

Second Edition 2019

No part of this book may be reproduced, stored in a retrieval system or transmitted in any form or means electronic, mechanical, photocopying, recording or otherwise, without prior written permission from Apa Publications.

Every effort has been made to provide accurate information in this publication, but changes are inevitable. The publisher cannot be responsible for any resulting loss, inconvenience or injury.

## DISTRIBUTION

**UK, Ireland and Europe**
Apa Publications (UK) Ltd
sales@insightguides.com
**United States and Canada**
Ingram Publisher Services
ips@ingramcontent.com
**Australia and New Zealand**
Woodslane
info@woodslane.com.au
**Southeast Asia**
Apa Publications (Singapore) Pte
singaporeoffice@insightguides.com
**Worldwide**
Apa Publications (UK) Ltd
sales@insightguides.com

## SPECIAL SALES, CONTENT LICENSING AND COPUBLISHING

Insight Guides can be purchased in bulk quantities at discounted prices. We can create special editions, personalised jackets and corporate imprints tailored to your needs.
sales@insightguides.com
www.insightguides.biz

# INDEX

---

## MAP LEGEND

| | |
|---|---|
| ● Start of tour | ★ Place of interest |
| ↠ Tour & route direction | ⓘ Tourist information |
| ❶ Recommended sight | ⚑ Statue/monument |
| ❷ Recommended restaurant/café | ✉ Main post office |
| | 🚌 Main bus station |
| | ◩ MRT station |
| | ⋇ Viewpoint |

| | |
|---|---|
| Park | |
| Important building | |
| Hotel | |
| Transport hub | |
| Market/store | |
| Pedestrian area | |
| Urban area | |

# INSIGHT ⊙ GUIDES

# OFF THE SHELF

Since 1970, INSIGHT GUIDES has provided a unique perspective on the world's best travel destinations by using specially commissioned photography and illuminating text written by local authors.

Whether you're planning a city break, a walking tour or the journey of a lifetime, our superb range of guidebooks and phrasebooks will inspire you to discover more about your chosen destination.

## INSIGHT GUIDES

offer a unique combination of stunning photos, absorbing narrative and detailed maps, providing all the inspiration and information you need.

## PHRASEBOOKS & DICTIONARIES

help users to feel at home, when away. Pocket-sized with a free app to download, they go where you do.

## CITY GUIDES

pack hundreds of great photos into a smaller format with detailed practical information, so you can navigate the world's top cities with confidence.

## EXPLORE GUIDES

feature easy-to-follow walks and itineraries in the world's most exciting destinations, with our choice of the best places to eat and drink along the way.

## POCKET GUIDES

combine concise information on where to go and what to do in a handy compact format, ideal on the ground. Includes a full-colour, fold-out map.

## EXPERIENCE GUIDES

feature offbeat perspectives and secret gems for experienced travellers, with a collection of over 100 ideas for a memorable stay in a city.

## www.insightguides.com